OXF

FOLK
TALES

OXFORDSHIRE
FOLK
TALES

KEVAN MANWARING

First published 2012

The History Press
The Mill, Brimscombe Port
Stroud, Gloucestershire, GL5 2QG
www.thehistorypress.co.uk

British Library Cataloguing in Publication Data.
A catalogue record for this book is available from the British Library.

ISBN 978 0 7524 6414 5

Typesetting and origination by The History Press
Printed in Great Britain

CONTENTS

ACKNOWLEDGEMENTS

Thank you to: Jennifer Horsfall (for her support and good listening skills); Anthony Nanson and Kirsty Hartsiotis (for conjuring spirits of place with me); Karola Renard and Mark Hassall (turning the wheel in Bonn); David Phelps (for kick-starting this great series); David Metcalfe (host of the Bath Storytelling Circle); Wayland the Skald (forging words at the Smithy); all the tellers and the listeners over the centuries who have kept these tales alive; Matilda Richards and The History Press; and Oxfordshire – for being such an inspiring county.

INTRODUCTION

As a child and young man growing up in Northampton, Oxfordshire was the 'special world' – in contrast to my very 'ordinary' one – just over the county border. Beyond what seemed (at the time) like a prosaic place to live, things got more picturesque and interesting in a south-westerly direction: the beautiful spire of Bloxham was a heartening site as one wended down the winding lanes towards the Cotswolds. Red brick turned to golden limestone. Banbury became my 'Bree' – and the Prancing Pony was the fine lady upon her cock horse, now immortalised in a splendid statue by the Cross. The Rollright Stones were the first stone circle I came to know; the nearest Neolithic monument to home, the first glimpse of prehistory and another way of being. I have visited it many times, and have had several magical moments there, often quietly communing with the Whispering Knights, the King's Stone or the King's Men. These ancient gnarled menhirs acted as kindling to my imagination.

The further south-west one went, the prettier it seemed to get. The charming towns of Chipping Norton, Stow-on-the-Wold, Burford and Moreton-in-Marsh waited. The hills got more dramatic – the Fosseway providing a free rollercoaster on my two wheels, as I crisscrossed the county countless times, visiting my old home town from the West Country where I settled in my late twenties. From Bath, and later, Stroud, the route across the Cotswolds was always my way back to my roots, and so I have probably traversed Oxfordshire more than any other county in England. It has become familiar to me, but still retains that special 'threshold' quality – it is a zone of transition for me, abutting as it does both my old home county (Northamptonshire) and my new one (Gloucestershire): near enough to be familiar, but far enough to be deemed as a place with a numinous atmosphere.

Sacred places that seem attainable have always held a special allure for me – my favourite stories are, so often, because the 'gateway' they provide seems imminent and accessible (e.g. in *Mythago Wood* by Robert Holdstock, Ryhope Wood – a small fragment of ancient woodland which feels tantalisingly close – could be Yardley Chase, an outlier of a wildwood that once stretched to the south coast). As I child 'I longed for scenes where man has never trod', as I followed in the footsteps of peasant poet, John Clare, who was interred in my home town. Exploring my neck of the woods – the 'spinneys' and gentle hills that demarcated the edge of my world – I searched for secret pathways; for roads less travelled.

In the selection of these stories I have eschewed the mainstream and explored the green lanes and hollow-ways of Oxfordshire's oral tradition – as recorded by the likes of Ruth Tongue and Katherine M. Briggs, who lived in the area. On my two wheels, or on two feet, I have visited all the places featured, often several times. Some, like the White Horse of Uffington, have been engraved upon my soul from years of pilgrimage (I once walked the Ridgeway to it – and beyond – to Avebury). If there is a good folk tale I have pounced upon it, and done my best to revivify it in my own voice – this has often followed a live performance. My preferred methodology was to strip the tale down to the 'bones' and then perform it to an audience, before committing it to a text version. If this was not possible, I have, at the very least, 'performed' it to myself – many times in situ, as a way of giving thanks to the original source of inspiration and checking that the tale evokes the spirit of the place accurately. Two significant shows where these tales were road-tested were: the 'Turning the Wheel', a bilingual storytelling performance which took place with fellow tellers Karola Renard, Mark Hassall and Anthony Nanson at Bonn

Central Library, Germany, on Twelfth Night, 5th of January 2012; and 'Spirits of Place', with Anthony Nanson (*Gloucestershire Folk Tales*) and Kirsty Hartsiotis (*Wiltshire Folk Tales*) at Hawkwood College, near Stroud, on St George's Day, 23rd of April, the same year. Others were tested at the Bath Storytelling Circle and similar events. Thus, the narrative style is informed by an authentic and individualistic style of oral delivery. I hope this brings them alive on the page, but does not exclude the reader/teller to perform them in their own way.

Where only a scrap or two of folklore existed I have fermented it in my imagination to create a folk tale around it. This, I feel, is exactly the process that storytellers have been engaged in over the millennia. The first 'versions' of these tales were possibly created in just the same way; an unusual feature or phenomenon providing the grit in the oyster to the local fabulist. Nature abhors a vacuum and so does the human imagination and where there is a lack of facts, we have an instinct to fill in the gaps with narrative invention ('Here be dragons'). I haven't imposed a story of my own upon a place, only selecting places that already have a folkloric focal point. My imagining of the tale of place is merely an addition to the secretion of narrative I have found already occurring there, a conversation I have joined in with. And in this way, the landscape is mythologised and the storytellers who have inhabited this county (and been inhabited by it) conjure a dreamtime from the windings of the rainbow serpent of the tongue, the hearth, the heart and the listener's attention. The traditional and contemporary merge in the moment of the telling. The ancient becomes topical. The 'there' becomes 'here'; the 'then' becomes the 'now'. We become part of the tale and the tale becomes a part of us.

Having learnt these stories to recreate in an extempore fashion, organically, in the moment, I feel I have a 'moveable county' within me now: my own version of Oxfordshire – selective, subjective; coloured, no doubt, by my predilections and peccadilloes. It feels like an interesting place to visit and I'll keep returning there, every time I tell one of these tales.

If this collection whets your appetite and encourages you to explore the county and become your own 'folk tale hunter', then it will have succeeded. May it deepen your appreciation of what is a beautiful area, the very quintessence of England – a mead-pit for kings and warriors; saints and scholars; highwaymen and rogues; ghosts and cavaliers; merchants and tinkers; future prime ministers and presidents; wise women and wizards; mistresses and storytellers – the crossroads of history where treasure can be found in both the great and the small; the lauded and the neglected; the glimmering fragment in the hedgerow; the time-worn feature, hiding in plain sight.

X marks the spot.

Kevan Manwaring, Stroud, 2012

Illustrations

The map on page 13 (with the exception of the coat of arms) and all line drawing illustrations are by the author (© 2012).

Oxfordshire

WARWICKSHIRE

NORTHAMPTONSHIRE

GLOUCESTERSHIRE

Long Compton

Cropredy
Sulgrave
Banbury

Bloxham
Adderbury

Rollright Stones

Chipping Norton

Bicester

Chastleton

Woodstock

Leafield

Burford

Otmoor

BUCKINGHAMSHIRE

Minster Lovell

Yarnton

Wychwood Bersy

Witney Blenheim

Stanton Harcourt

Oxford

Garsington

Thame

Faringdon

Abingdon

Dorchester -on-Thames

Clifton Hampden

Whitenham Clumps

Kingston Lisle

Sutton Courtenhay

Uffington Wantage

Didcot

Henley-on-Thames

Goring

Stoke Row

WILTSHIRE

BERKSHIRE

As I was Going to Banbury

As I was going to Banbury
Ri-fol la-ti-tee O
As I was going to Banbury
I saw a fine codling apple tree
With a ri-fol la-ti-tee O

And when the codlings began to fall
Ri-fol la-ti-tee O
And when the codlings began to fall
I found five hundred men in all.
With a ri-fol la-ti-tee O.

And one of the men I saw was dead,
Ri-fol la-ti-tee O
And one of the men I saw was dead
So I sent for a hatchet to open his head.
With a ri-fol la-ti-tee O.

And in his head I found a spring,
Ri-fol la-ti-tee O
And in his head I found a spring
And seven young salmon a-learning to sing
With a ri-fol la-ti-tee O.

And one of the salmon as big as I,
Ri-fol la-ti-tee O
And one of the salmon as big as I
Now do you not think I am telling a lie?
With a ri-fol la-ti-tee O.

And one of the salmon as big as an elf,
Ri-fol la-ti-tee O
And one of the salmon as big as an elf –
If you want any more you must sing it yourself
With a ri-fol la-ti-tee O

One

RIDE A COCK HORSE

Ride a cock horse to Banbury Cross,
To see a Fyne lady ride on a white horse.
With rings on her fingers and bells on her toes,
She shall have music wherever she goes.

This place has always been a crossing way, where things … pass over. Nowadays it is little more than a glorified roundabout, with a steady stream of traffic circling it, belching exhaust fumes. An elegant statue watches on, but few stop and stare – the busy people are always rushing somewhere. Yet it has always been thus – for centuries folk have passed this way, from west to south bringing salt along the Salt Way, from Droitwich to London, the Welsh Marches to Romney Marsh, and Banbury Lane, running from Hamtun along the Fosse Way to Stow-on-the-Wold; men trading goods or blows. Many armies have marched this way – Iron Age warriors; Roman centurions; Saxons, settling by the Cherwell; a band of Danes once, coming from Hamtun, ravaged the county, until they settled and learnt the value of peace. Banbury Castle, a Royalist stronghold, was besieged in the Civil War and finally pulled down, 500 years since its construction. And the three crosses which the town once had – High Cross, where important proclamations were made; the Bread Cross, where the bakers and butchers sold their wares, and bread was doled out to the poor on Good Friday; and the White Cross. The town worthies decided the populace had 'far gone into Puritanism' and had the High Cross pulled down, to curtail the Catholic pilgrims who came to the town. Just after dawn on the 26th of July 1600, two masons began demolishing the High Cross, with a crowd of at least 100 men looking on. When the spire fell to the ground Henry Shewell cried out jubilantly, 'God be thanked, their god Dagon is fallen down to the ground!' The Bread Cross and the White Cross were destroyed in the same year.

Banbury – famous for 'cheese, cakes and zeal', so the saying goes, and you can see why.

And yet, despite their efforts, the true crossing place remained – silent and unseen to all but those with subtle eyes. Only on a moonlit night was it possible to catch a glimpse of the fine lady. In the deadness of the dark, listen sharp and you might hear her music. But stop your ears with wax, lest you want the rings on her fingers and bells on her toes to lead you away to the land of Fey – never to be seen again by your loved ones. They say her beauty is spellbinding. Once you see her, you are enchanted by her comeliness.

Every year, the townsfolk process through the town with their hobby horses to keep on her good side. She likes to be honoured; some would say placated.

Some say it was Queen Bess herself who was the 'fine lady', Spencer's Faerie Queene. She had travelled to Banbury to see a cross being erected. Banbury was situated at the top of a steep hill and in order to help carriages up the steep incline a white cock horse, a large stallion, was made available by the town's council to help with this task. When the Queen's carriage attempted to go up the hill a wheel broke and the Queen chose to mount the cock horse and ride to the Banbury cross. The people of the town had decorated the cock horse with ribbons and bells and provided minstrels to accompany her so 'she shall have music wherever she goes'.

And there are other theories, but all let the truth slip through their hands – like Rhiannon, who rode a white horse and would not let herself be caught until she chose; like her older sister, Epona, Celtic horse goddess; like the Queen of Elfland herself. And Tam Lin would agree – that you would not want to meet her at the witching hour. He crossed over, but Janet won him back:

> Just at the mirk and midnight hour
> The fairy folk will ride,
> And they that would their true-love win,
> At Miles Cross they must bide.

So, take care if you pass this Crossing Place at an in-between time. Pay your respects to the fine lady, and go quickly on your way. If you do not pay your respects, she will exact her tithe at a terrible cost – as a good doctor, William Oldys, once found out…

Doctor Oldys was a vicar at New College. During the Civil War, even men of the cloth were not immune to the madness which swept the land. All were forced to make a hard choice – one that split families apart. Oldys was loyal to the King, and so found himself the natural enemy of Cromwell and his rebel army. As a consequence, it was no longer safe for him and his family to stay at home at his fine vicarage in Adderbury, next to one of the finest

spires in the county. Oldys decided it was prudent to make for
Banbury, which was a garrison for the King at that time. The preparations were made – Oldys would go first and secure dwellings for
them; then he would return to rendezvous with his wife and son
(whom he intended to get to the safety of the university) on the
road at an appointed day and hour.

Word of this plan was somehow leaked to the enemy – by a
nefarious turncoat neighbour. And thus, some Parliamentarian
soldiers lay in wait for the good doctor as he made his way to meet
his wife and child.

Yet Oldys had made plans for such an eventuality – for difficult
times make for cautious hearts. His wife and son would ride out to
the spot first, for any soldiers would not attack them. If they met
troops, they were to give him a signal – if the men be of the King's
party his good wife would hold up her gloved hand and he would
approach; if not, she must pass on without further sign.

And so the good doctor found himself anxiously waiting in the
green shadows as he watched his wife and son approach the spot.
As he feared, a cavalry appeared in the clearing, breastplates and
spears glinting in the light through the trees.

As the doctor's wife approached the men, trying not to show her
terror, she saw they were Roundheads and rode straight on, with
only the slightest of polite acknowledgements to them. Their hard
eyes scrutinised her from behind their iron veils.

The doctor, duly noting that no hand was raised, made a hasty
retreat back to Banbury. The enemy noticed his sudden departure
and gave chase with alacrity. On their chargers they rapidly gained
ground. To delay them, the doctor scattered his purse along the
trail – but there was one amongst them who desired blood more
than gold and would not tarry for the mud-tainted coin. He had
known the good doctor and had received his charity, but this did
not soften his heart. Cromwell had replaced Christ in his heart.

As the good doctor passed his former abode on the way to
Banbury, his horse stopped, thinking it was home. With mounting
desperation, Oldys could not get it to move forward by any persua-
sion. This gave the enemy time to overtake him and, apprehending

him, they did not hesitate to exact their fateful toll – one pulled a pistol and shot the good doctor dead. It was noted afterwards, by neighbours of the parish, that the one who had warned the troops fell down dead on the very spot the doctor was slain.

At New College, a tablet in memory of Doctor William Oldys was raised, recording how he was murdered by the Rebels.

* * *

Visit Banbury today and you'll see a statue of the fine lady by the Cross. A blood-thirsty horse goddess, the ultimate nightmare; or an elfin Queen, comely and fair? She is all these things and more, immortal and ever changing. Perhaps she is sufficiently honoured, and travellers who pass that way may feel safe – or perhaps not!

The presence of this Fine Lady is a gift to any storyteller. Although there is a possibility that she is none other than one of the Oxfordshire Fiennes (whose famous descendants include an explorer father and two actor sons) and her cock horse is nothing more than the strong stallion used to pull her carriage up the hill into town, I have used my artistic license to interpret her as the Queen of Elfland – the 'rings on her fingers and bells on her toes' are akin to the bridle of the one who graced Thomas the Rhymer with her presence (decorated with 'fifty silver bells and nine…'). Enchanting music was often heard before the appearance of the Fey, and any who heard it was doomed to go there, or fade away in this world. Its pull is irresistible, as W.B. Yeats captured so immortally in his classic poem The Stolen Child: *'Come away, O human child, to the waters and the wild…'*

Fairyland might seem far away from Banbury, but since this was the first town outside of Northampton (my old home county)

I would come across as I ventured 'into the west', I think of it as a 'Lud-in-the-Mist' type place (the town in Hope Mirrlees' 1926 novel which borders Faerie), being the gateway into the Cotswolds and beyond to the 'weird' West Country and wilder Wales. Here, I have melded two strands of folklore together – one about the Queen of Elfland and crossroads (as featured in the Scottish ballad 'Tam Lin'); and the other a local folk tale about William Oldys. In this coupling of the mythic and the mundane something magical occurs. One needs to be anchored to the other – to stop the former flying away into the ether and the latter from being stuck in the mud of reality. Visit Banbury on the day of the Hobby Horse Fair in early July, when unusual beasts from all over England gather for a procession through town, culminating in the People's Park, and you will see this occurring before your eye. For a while, reality bends.

Two

The White Horse of Uffington

Come to the Horse Fair-O – have you a scrape and thrill!
Come to the White Horse, stabled on Uffington Hill.

It was the time of the Scouring of the Horse, a great fair that took place every seven years on Uffington Hill. The local lord himself had funded it, though much did he rue the fact, complaining about the state of the economy, taxes and poor harvests. But the spirit of the people to celebrate could not be suppressed, especially when they'd had to wait so long; long enough for legs to grow, and tales in the telling of the previous fair. Littl'uns who'd grown up listening to what the grown-ups spun were now eager to discover the magic for themselves. Would it be real, or moonbeams on the chalk? Well the day had finally come…

Uffington Fair is always a very lively affair – officially lasting for three days – although the revelry often continues before and after with the quaffing of much ale, the feasting, the cheese-rolling down into The Manger, stalls selling gewgaws and local wares, wrestling, dancing, tests of strength, the sharing of news and views, and, of course, the Scouring of the Horse. The villagers took great pride in this, and Betty was one of them – a local lass, this was the second Scouring she could remember. She was con-ceived at one, fourteen years ago, so her folks remind her, much to her embarrassment: she was an 'Uffington gal, thru and thru,' her Dad said. The fair had always seemed magical to her, with its many sights and wonders, but especially this year when she felt… different, and had taken great care in preparing her outfit, a lovely clean white dress with ornate bonnet, her best shoes, her hair done just so, and her face 'as fresh and comely as a May morn-ing', as her Granny said. Holding a garland of flowers, she had proudly joined in the procession to the Horse at dawn along with the whole village – apart from Granny, whose legs weren't like they used to be.

Bill the butcher led the way, beating his pigskin drum in solemn manner, his black tricorne hat sporting a pheasant feather, 'like the cock o' the morn,' someone giggled, until elbowed into respectful silence.

They gathered in a great circle round the chalk figure – over three hundred feet in length – which was carved into the side of the Downs. They stood overlooking the Vale of the White Horse, slowly emerging from the mist as though from the dawn of time.

The drumming stopped and the priest said a few words, blessing the Scouring in the name of the Lord; and then they set to work, removing any weeds that had grown in the chalk over the last few years. It was said if the Horse grew too hairy, the harvest would falter: 'No grain in the barn; no butter for the bairn.' And so the villagers took the Scouring seriously – as long as the White Horse shone down upon them 'luck would fill the Vale'. So the old ones said, and so the young 'uns followed. And so it always had been – longer than any could remember.

As Betty pulled out the tufts, a laugh caught her attention; it was John, the blacksmith's son, with his dark lick of hair. He gave her a wink, and she blushed even more.

They spent the rest of the Scouring coyly flirting with each other. It was like playing in the smithy – Betty knew it was perilous and she could easily get her fingers burnt, but she could not resist. There was something about the day, the time of year, and the time of her life. Like the verdant land around her, she felt like she was … waking up.

The June sun was burning away the mist to reveal fields brimming with new growth. With so many hands at work, the Scouring was soon complete. A festival breakfast awaited them – warm bread and strong cheese, spring onions and last year's apple chutney – which they took on the flanks of the hill. A cool jug of cider was passed around and for the first time, handed to Betty, who warily took a sip and coughed. John laughed his easy laugh, accepted it from her and downed a draught, wiping the back of his hand with a smack of his lips. They smiled at each other as someone struck up a fiddle.

'Come on!' John led them, laughing, to the delights of the fair.

* * *

What a day it had been! They were deliciously weary from it now – all the delights they had seen and savoured, the rickety fairground rides, the side-stalls, the sugary treats, the buzz of conversation, the dancing and foolery. With a satisfied sigh, they wandered away from the fair, which was now being packed away.

The villagers lingered on the hillside, savouring the last golden drops of the day.

A little awkward, the young couple held hands and walked away from the crowd.

From the ramparts of the 'castle' – the earthwork above the Horse – they watched the sun set. Below, the Horse gleamed in the silver light of the moon which rose as the sun fell.

Around them they sensed the gaggles of villagers, making merry. Louder than all, they could hear old Lob, the local teller in his flow now he was lubricated with cider. He was declaiming on his favourite subject of horse lore: 'If mares slipped their foals, a black donkey would be run with them to cure evil; if a donkey was unavailable then a goat could be used the same way!' Laughter carried across the hillside.

'What about different coloured horses, Lob – what do you make of that?' someone piped up, with a nudge and a wink to a friend.

'A good horse is never a bad colour.' Sounds of affirmation, though one scratched his head.

'A horse with a white flash on its forehead is lucky, as is a white-footed one, but if it has four white feet they should be avoided, it'll be unlucky with a surly humour.'

Someone commented, 'We'd best be careful then, with the White Horse so close!' Lob rubbished this idea.

'Of all the horses, a pure white horse is the most auspicious – but its magic is strong, and so it is wise to cross 'uns fingers, and keep 'em crossed 'til ye see a dog.' Nearby a dog barked, and everyone laughed with relief.

Snuggled on his coat, John and Betty lay in the twilight, holding one another. Betty tingled all over. This was the first time she'd been close to a man. The first time she had slept outdoors. But since half the village was there, it felt safe and acceptable to do so. It was common for them to sleep out on Horse Fair Hill on this special night. Many a good memory had been forged on its flanks, and passed down the generations, making the young 'uns especially keen to have their own 'experience'.

The cider, the music, the stars – all swirled in her mind. Betty felt like she could float off, but John's arms softly held her to the earth. His gentle words soothed her, his rough hand smoothing her hair.

As he cradled her in his arms, John told her how on moonlit nights just like this, the Horse would come down to feed in the Manger – the meadow in the hollow of the hill beneath them. This made Betty shiver and she was glad of his strong arms around her. It had been a rich day in many ways – she'd had a bit too much to eat and drink, and her head was whirling as she found herself slipping into a deep slumber, the sound of Uffington Fair drifting on the night air.

* * *

The distant beat of the drums carried her deep into the hillside which seemed to open up and swallow her, until she felt like the land itself. She felt the stirring of every living thing – beetle and ladybird, mole and vole, rabbit and hare, fox and badger, swine and stag – moving above her and inside her. So much life! Sowing and growing, mating and decaying – an endless cycle that stretched back a long, long time.

The drumming became the thudding of horse hooves, and suddenly she was above ground, galloping along – a white horse, as pale as moonlight! She ran free across the Downs, along the Ridgeway, its ancient paths glowing in the silver light. Whinnying with joy, she came out onto the open land above the White Horse – which, strangely, was not there. Only a clean swathe of grass could be seen. Her nostrils quivered and she snorted a plume of breath. The landscape was the same, but different. The Castle was surrounded by a palisade of sharpened timbers, dark spikes against the lights of a village inside. The strong wooden gates creaked open and out processed a line of people holding torches, led by drummers and priests and priestesses in white robes, adorned by oak leaves and flowers. They made their way to the side of the hill and the drumming suddenly fell silent.

As one, they watched as the moon rose in her fullness, flooding the Manger with unearthly light. The robed ones began to speak in a strange tongue that sounded vaguely familiar.

Betty could catch the odd word, which echoed in the back of her mind like a pebble dropped in a deep well. They turned to her and for a moment she was frightened, thinking they had spotted her, the trespasser; but they hailed her by a strange name: 'Epona!' The tribe came forward and placed offerings at her feet – the bounty of the land. And then the priesthood oversaw the cutting of the turf. By their direction, the shape of the Horse was carved out of the hillside, revealing the chalk beneath. The design was stylised and elegant, and resembled the intricate ornaments some wore, or the tattoos revealed as men stripped down to their waists to work on the Horse. Finally, it was complete and the moon-glow bestowed upon it an unearthly sentience. Betty felt the spirit of her horse pour into it. The Goddess was happy and lay upon the bed they had prepared for her. She felt soothed by the songs the tribe sang, the fellowship that flowed around the gathering – a circle of love, binding them together.

* * *

Betty awoke, blinking, yawning and rubbing her eyes. The ghost of the sun could be sensed through the mist, which lay like a white sea over the Vale. Somewhere, a cock crowed and around her lay the huddled shapes of villagers, looking like no more than bundles of clothes by smouldering fires.

She was a little disorientated at first, and unsettled by her vivid dream. But it was all right. John still held her in his solid arms, snoring lightly.

Below her, the White Horse of Uffington lay; a reassuring permanence on the landscape. It was old, very old, and yet it had survived. The people of the Vale of the White Horse had preserved it for all of these years; beyond living memory – but not the memory of the land.

Around her, villagers were awakening and returning to their homes, to their chores and tasks. Uffington Fair was over for another seven years, but Betty would remember it for the rest of her life. She had been changed by her night on the hill. The horse inside her had woken up, had tasted the Manger, and would not be put back in its stable.

Beside her, John stirred, yawned and smiled. He brushed down his coat and put it round her shoulders and off they set.

'Well, that's it then; back to the forge for I,' said John. 'May the Horse bring us luck.'

Both were lost in their thoughts, the ghost of the night lingering. Seven years! Who knows what life will bring them by then?

Betty knew and she walked with a confident gait down the hill, arm-in-arm with John, her bridegroom-to-be. Although, he did not know it yet.

The White Horse of Uffington is an iconic image of the area. Whenever I travel by train between London and the West County I always notice it. When I have returned from a trip abroad it is a heartening sight – I know I am back in England, its very heart. I always breathe a sigh of relief when the claustrophobic sprawl of the capital and its hinterland gives way to a gentler, greener landscape. Once the threshold of Old Father Thames is crossed things become more mythic. Entering the Vale of the White Horse, the countryside widens out into a broad valley, the hills of the Ridgeway rising to the south. The White Horse feels like a threshold guardian of sorts, and perhaps that was the intention of the original makers. It was long believed King Alfred cut it to celebrate his victory over the Danes – in that role he was being England's threshold guardian – but the horse actually dates back to 2800 BCE. It might well have marked the tribal territory of the area, or had some religious significance: a horse cult; or horse tribe. I like to imagine that J.R.R. Tolkien, the county's greatest storyteller, would have been inspired by the sight to create the horse lords of Middle Earth, the Rohan – perhaps while standing on Faringdon Folly (on a clear day, you can see the Horse from there), which is rather like Saruman's tower,

Isengard. The iconic chalk figure stirs the imagination (as it did for my friend Peter Please, who wrote The Chronicles of the White Horse *– a children's novel, accompanied by an album of quintessentially English folk music). Although no actual folk tale exists, I took the rags of folk lore connected to it – chiefly around the Scouring Fair, which used to be held every seven years – and wove them into a story which I hope evokes the spirit of place. Like young Betty, I too have slept out there (within Uffington Castle itself – the sacred flanks of the White Horse is not a place to pitch a tent). I cannot remember the dreams I had there, but I imagine they were vivid. As a young man I came across the notion that by sleeping or meditating at sacred sites we can 'time travel' and catch a glimpse of their past, perhaps tapping into 'place memory'. Do the events that happen at a site become recorded somehow? Certainly, battle-fields feel that way, and haunted houses. And so I adopted this 'shamanic' method of narrative retrieval.*

Any location can be explored in this way – dreaming the land – there's certainly no harm in trying, and even if no apparent evidence remains of its 'story' we can perhaps retrieve fragments with our 'dream-soundings'.

Certainly, listening to the Earth is a good place to start. How else can we tell the deeper story of a land? As with the cutting of the Horse into the chalk beneath the turf, the deeper you go, the more is revealed. If we limit ourselves to what is only visible on the surface (or in books and archives; virtual or otherwise) then we can miss so much.

The real story is always the one right under our feet.

Three

DRAGON HILL

It is lonely being a dragon in England. Most of your kin have been killed off by knights eager to prove themselves and win the hands of maidens. Many a local hero wants to make his name for being a dragon-slayer and many a sleepy village boasts at having defeated a dragon – which remains on in names such as the village of Worminghall. A sensitive dragon could be easily upset by the many images of dragon-slaying depicted in churches and civic windows – a legion of St Michaels slaying numerous cousins; or a squadron of St Patricks casting out Irish relatives. The most famous dragon-slaying saint is, of course, St George himself – England's patron saint – who was born in what is now modern day central Turkey. It seems unlikely that this Turkish knight ended up on the gentle Downs of Oxfordshire, but that is what we are expected to believe with regards to Dragon Hill, the low conical mound over-looked by the White Horse of Uffington. Where wayward dragons linger surely errant knights can too. Suspend your disbelief and listen to the tale of George and the Dragon…

* * *

Jorgio was a pork butcher from Cappadocia – a town where nothing ever seemed to happen. Every day he would make sausages and he would chop them up; make and chop; make and chop. And he was fed up. He knew he was destined for greater things – but he wasn't exactly sure what.

Then one day, when he was mincing beef, it came to him; he would become a dragon-slayer! The fact that he didn't know the first thing about slaying dragons, or even where to find them, was a mere detail. He would work it out as he went along. And so, to the amazement and amusement of his friends and family, he sold up his butcher's business, bought a suit of armour and a spear, and set off – in search of adventure.

As he stopped at the famous 'fairy chimneys' of his homeland to break his fast with … sausage … he wondered if he had done the right thing. Still, he girded his loins for a long ride. 'Come on, old girl. Giddy up!'

Well, it just so happened at this time – as so often happens in these stories – that a town became afflicted with a 'dragon-infes-tation'. The town was in Libya, Northern Africa, and there's some would say it was because of their 'desert-heathen' ways that they were afflicted so – yet it might just have been bad luck. Whatever the cause, the fact was they were forced to sacrifice sheep to placate the serpent; yet its appetite was ravenous and they were soon running out of livestock. This could not carry on! Desperate times call for desperate measures. It was decided lots would be drawn, and a human sacrifice chosen from amongst the citizens of the realm each full moon to keep the dragon happy. Yet, as you can imagine, such a state of affairs did not make the townsfolk happy, as mother was forced to say goodbye to daughter; father to son. It was hard for the dwindling populace, living under the shadow of the dragon.

The Princess of the realm thought this was awfully unfair, because the Royal family were exempt from the lottery. Her fair brow crinkling into a frown, one day the princess said, 'Papa, why is it only the poor people of the realm get to put their names in the lots? Isn't that awfully unfair?'

'My child, how naïve you are! That's the way of things and be grateful that it's not your pretty little neck on the line.'

But the Princess, Virtuous by name, virtuous by nature, insisted on having her name placed with the rest – she slipped it in secretly – and to everyone's horror, as luck would have it, her name was chosen! And there was nothing the King could do about it, without causing a riot.

To her credit, the Princess did not complain – she accepted her fate, and so found herself on the dragon mound, tied to a stake, awaiting her fate. 'Oh bother!' she said, pouting her pretty lips.

Just then, Jorgio rode into town. It had taken him a long time to find a town terrorised by a living, breathing dragon – there seemed to be a terrible shortage of them; indeed, they could be considered an endangered species – but that did not matter to Jorgio. For him, it was an appointment with destiny.

He rode up to the foot of the hill, dismounted and tethered his whickering horse at a safe distance. He then took his spear and set to work. He climbed the hill and declaimed: 'Have no fear, Princess, I am here, Jorgio the Dragon-Slayer!' He thrust his spear into the hill and stood guard.

She looked him up and down sceptically. 'Have you killed many dragons before?'

'No, this is my first…' the knight replied, glad his helmet hid his burning cheeks.

'Hmm,' pouted the Princess petulantly. She did not reckon on her chances much.

As the day turned to night, dusk came – the time when the dragon emerged to feed. And sure enough it did – sliding out of the hole at the bottom of the hill, and slithering around and around until it rose up before … a knight in shining armour standing between it and dinner! It was furious. Rearing up, it attacked; snapping and hissing at the knight, who ducked this way and that, jabbing with his spear. It was all fangs, wings and hot-breath and Jorgio had a hard time fending it off, his spear not having much effect. He couldn't keep this up! What was he to do?

Suddenly, the Princess piped up: 'Oh, brave knight, my garter! Take my garter!'

'My lady, we haven't the time for that now. Can't you see I'm busy?'

'No, you silly man! My garter has magical powers – use it to defeat the dragon!'

'Why didn't you say so before?'

'A girl's got to have some secrets…'

So, Jorgio quickly slipped the garter from her leg and, using it like a lassoo, caught the dragon around the neck. Instantly, it went docile and lay down at the Princess' feet like a pet dog.

The dragon defeated, Jorgio untied the Princess and received a lovely peck on the cheek for his efforts.

'My hero!'

Bowing low, which is hard to do in armour, Jorgio said: 'At your service, my Lady.'

Then, together, they led the dragon down the hill like a dog on a lead. They walked into the town with it, gathering people on the way, until they arrived at the town square. There, Jorgio addressed the crowd – by now the whole population was there.

'Good people! You need fear no longer. The dragon has been defeated – by the Sword of the Lord.'

A small boy said, 'But it's not dead!'

'The dragon has been defeated, as you can see before you.'

'Yes, by the power of my garter!' muttered the Princess.

Losing patience, Jorgio cut off the head of the dragon.

'The dragon has been defeated ... by the Sword of the Lord!' He lifted the bloody head before them and they all fell to their knees, and it was said they all converted to the one true faith there and then.

And thus the legend of the dragon-slayer, the good Christian knight, was born. Jorgio's fame spread across the Middle East as he converted more and more souls.

What became of the Princess, those ancient and forgetful story-tellers do not record.

Yet it seems the dragon was to have the last laugh, or roar – for Jorgio was captured in Palestine by the Serpent King, Gevya Garsa, and was unfortunately executed, suffering the triple-death of the martyr: he was forced to walk in red-hot iron shoes; then broken on a wheel; and, finally, immersed in quicklime (for good measure).

Yet, where his broken body was cast, in Lydda, a shrine was raised. Here, his memory was worshipped. And centuries later it was this very shrine that the Crusaders came across on their way to the Holy Land. It had already been a long, difficult and costly war – they needed something to shore up their flagging campaign, so the Crusaders adopted the dragon-slayer – now a saint – carrying his image into battle, wearing his colours of white and red in the Gulf.

And though the Crusade was not entirely successful, the Crusaders brought back the icon of Saint George, as he became known, and carried on his legend.

His popularity grew and it was decided in AD 1222, at the Council of Oxford, to make his feast day, April 23rd, a national celebration. But it wasn't until the fourteenth century, nearly a thousand years after his death in Lydda, in AD 303, that he was made patron saint of England – when the Order of the Garter was formed in his memory.

And so, to this day, we celebrate that pork butcher from Cappadocia – our very own Turkish knight; and in these multi-cultural times, that's no bad thing.

So, let's hear it for Saint George! 'Cry God for Harry, England and Saint George!' as Shakespeare – whose birth and death day just so happens to be the 23rd of April, Saint George's Day – has Henry V cry at Agincourt.

And if you go to Uffington you'll see the low conical mound known as Dragon Hill, where it was said the blood of the dragon was spilled (somehow transferred from Libya …). And to this day, no grass grows upon it – so there must be a grain of truth in it, surely? And if that's not fanciful enough some folk believe the White Horse itself is not a horse, but a dragon, cut to commemorate the victory of our 'English dragon-slayer'. Take a walk upon these romantic hills and decide for yourself – for dragons will live in England as long as folk believe in them. Perhaps you'd like to adopt one, or start a sanctuary?

Although it seems unlikely that Saint George, let alone a dragon, set foot (or horny claw) in the county, the tradition of Dragon Hill (in itself a remarkable topographical feature) cannot be ignored. Stories attach themselves to such places. Humankind has been making up stories about the shapes in the land for a long time ('as old as the hills'). Dindsenchas, or stories of place, mythologise the landscape like the Dreamtime stories of the Aborigines. Every knoll or dell becomes numinous with narrative significance. A continuum of human/non-human relationship is created. The mythic transfigures the familiar and the secular becomes sacred. The top of Dragon Hill is certainly as bare as a monk's pate. It would make a good place to fight a dragon and rescue a maiden. Of course, England has its share of 'native' dragon tales (the Lambton Worm being the most famous) – whether they were introduced by waves of Germanic invaders (with their Nidhugs and Fafnirs); or if they were the result of the discovery of dinosaur bones; or whether the stories evoke the 'dragon in the land' (a geomantic earth energy), who knows? But here they remain, fossils of belief. And perhaps the fact the county flower is the Snake's Head Fritillary is no coincidence. Here, in Oxfordshire at least, there be dragons.

Four

WAYLAND
THE SMITH

Leave a silver coin for Wayland the Smith – there on the capstone in front of his house, the old long barrow they call Wayland's Smithy – and your horse will be shod by morn and the coin vanished like the stars at daybreak. This custom has been maintained for centuries – no one knows how long – and a good one it is too, as any passing tinker would tell you. It is easy enough to hide in the trees that line the Ridgeway – that ancient English road running alongside it – and wait 'til fortune smiles. It pays to perpetuate the legend with a rumour here, a tale there, to a stranger at a horse fair, or in a tavern. Everybody wins.

Tinkers have always been workers of metal, as their name suggests, and horses have always been their first love. Nomads from the east, they like to keep moving and earn a little on the way. The luck is passed along by little signs the normal folk would not notice. The price is sleeping rough at such a spooky spot – not much fun in the pouring rain. You have to be careful that your woodsmoke isn't noticed. It's hard to keep the chill out, but maybe it's more than the damp. The barrow is full of bones – the old stone glowering with angry ghosts.

Everyone has a tale to tell.

Sometimes, on a night when the sky seems to hold its breath, they speak. Cynics say it's just the wind soughing through the beech trees that stand like sentinels around the bone house – but stay there the night and see for yourself; feel the black air press in around you. Listen, listen to the Silent Ones.

At the back of the barrow, in the dark-most dark, a voice from the long ago waits to be heard…

* * *

Some say I acted out of revenge. I say I acted out of love. My name has become muddled up with so much nonsense over the centuries – like an impure alloy.

Let me tell you how it was.

Before I was a god I was a man, Volund, though of elfish blood it had to be said – and perhaps that called me to her. Sons of the King of the Finns, my two brothers, Egil and Slagfinn, and I spied three beautiful swan maidens bathing. Valkyries on holiday from selecting the fallen in battle or serving mead in Valhalla, they had taken off their swan down and slipped into the water. We grabbed their swan skins and 'persuaded' them to marry us. Tall and fair, high-breasted and strong-thighed, they were all lovely, but mine, Hervör-Alvitr, was the loveliest. She eventually seemed to accept her fate. She grew to love me, though it took patience – like taming a wild animal. We settled down to married life and we were happy.

But happiness never lasts.

After nine winters we awoke one morning to find the Valkyries had fled. They somehow had found their swan skins and flown away. My brothers, beside themselves, pursued – they put on their snow shoes and headed into the howling blizzard of the north.

I never saw them again.

My bride left me a ring forged of elfish craft from pure Rhine gold. I took this as a sign of her love. In her absence I made seven hundred replicas of it, hoping each time my beloved Hervör would appear. I joined the seven hundred rings together – the true one hidden amongst them, so that only I or my beloved could tell which. One night I discovered the true ring had been taken, which gave me hope that my sweetheart would return, but she never did.

I lost myself in my work. I made my craft my prayer – sweating at the forge, day after day. Nobody could turn metal like me.

Word of my skill, and of my ring hoard, reached King Nidud of Sweden. They caught me while I slumbered, exhausted from my toil. Nidud seized my wealth, and ordered me hamstrung and imprisoned on the island of Sævarstöð. There I was forced to forge items for the Thief-king – otherwise I would starve. I was even forced to make my own prison, a labyrinth.

My precious ring, Hervör's gift, was given to the King's only daughter, Bodvild.

Nidud appropriated Gram – the precious sword I forged. I swore vengeance on my captor and his kin. Every day I collected feathers to make a pair of wings with which I could escape when the time was right – white swan feathers. Perhaps my love had not forsaken me after all. A slender hope, but it kept me going during my imprisonment on that bleak island.

One day, the King came – the stolen sword needed mending. I cleverly forged an exact replica and replaced it without him noticing.

When the King's sons visited me in secret, overcome with hoard-greed, I did not hesitate in taking advantage of what the Norns had gifted me. I got them drunk and slaughtered them with their father's stolen sword. Then I used my skill to fashion goblets from their skulls; jewels from their eyes; and a brooch from their teeth. I sent the goblet to the King; the jewels to the Queen; and the brooch to the King's daughter – they were unaware of the nature of their treasures, even praising my skill. How clever was their tame slave, they prated. The trinkets had such a *shine* to them.

Then the Fates smiled again.

Bodvild took 'her' ring to me to be mended – my wife's ring. I seized it and, overcome by a rage, forced myself upon her. From that violent union came a son, so I hear, but I did not stick around to raise him. Escape was all that mattered.

There were enough feathers now. I forged a pair of wings with my skill and made my escape. Grasping my sword and the ring, I soared heavenward like Hervör, my love.

Freedom!

Yet I did not slink off like a coward, but returned to Nidud's palace to inform him of all that I had done – flying out of reach as I gloated. He ordered his archer, my own brother Egil, under enchantment, to shoot me down, but seeing it was his own sibling, Egil deliberately misfired and his arrow only burst a bladder of the King's sons' blood I had hidden on my person, which drenched the King. As he rained down curses upon me, I flew away, laughing.

I headed for Alf-heim, where I was finally reunited with my beloved bride and she agreed to be with me once again. Despite my lame leg, I continued plying my craft – magical swords and impenetrable suits of armour, forged by the 'crippled blacksmith of uncanny skill' – and a legend was born. All across the Northern Lands they honoured me. In Iceland a stone labyrinth is known as Volund's House. Perhaps this tradition inspired their Nordic cousins, the Danes, who settled in these isles to name the barrow on the Ridgeway, close by to the White Horse, Wayland's Smithy. Has a nice ring to it, doesn't it?

* * *

Day comes and the legends fade like mist in the sun, yet the wise know it is best to honour the Silent Ones. So, the next time you pass Wayland's House, leave a silver coin to the smith-god and whatever you need mending shall be forged afresh by morning.

Wayland's Smithy is one of my favourite prehistoric monuments – and it just so happens to be in Oxfordshire (these days). Of course, it is older than the respective counties of Oxfordshire or Berkshire, being five and a half thousand years old. The most recent evidence dates its earliest ritual use from between 3590 and 3555 BCE – pre-dating the surviving long barrow were remnants of a mortuary structure of stone and wood: 'On a pavement of sarsen stone slabs lay a narrow wooden box, into which people were successively placed. Two split tree-trunks were positioned upright at each end.' Later, the neolithic burial chamber was raised. The remains of fourteen people, comprising of eleven males, two females and a child, were discovered in the structure when it was excavated in 1963. New radiocarbon dating has shown that the first burials were probably placed there in 3590-3555 BCE, and the last in 3580-3550 BCE. The barrow was therefore used for no more than fifteen years – less than a single generation. It is also possible that the barrow was used for an even shorter period of time, perhaps just a year. After a period of between forty and one hundred years, the structure was covered by an oval mound of chalk and earth,

derived from two flanking ditches. This act signalled the closure of the barrow, but its significance was not forgotten. After a period of disuse, perhaps lasting twenty years, a second, larger barrow with a monumental façade was constructed over the top. Built between about 3,460 and 3,400 BCE, this trapezoidal mound had a kerb, façade and stone-lined transepted chamber. It absorbed the older mound altogether.

For millennia it remained a mystery, and it is no wonder many legends grew around it. Set back from the Ridgeway in its own whispering grove of beech, it is an uncanny place that doesn't feel quite part of this world. Of course, the legend of the mighty smith, Wayland, was imported from Norse Mythology. It might seem strange to hear this tale on the Chalk Downs of England, but clearly whoever named it after the wounded blacksmith did not find it so fanciful to associate the site with him. I, for one, feel the place deserves some respect and perhaps it is best to be on the safe side and leave an offering … just in case.

Once, I heard the Norse smith's tale in situ, related by the Oxford-based storyteller, Wayland (Matt Copley). I encouraged him to perform it when the storytellers we had gone there to see (scheduled to relate the tale, 'complete with anvil') failed to turn up. He performed it standing in the entrance to the barrow to a small crowd of visitors. It felt very resonant for him to be doing it there – in honour of his Skaldic namesake – paying his dues with the coin of his tale.

Five

THE RAVEN OF SINODUN HILL

It had been an accepted truth in the Vale that there was treasure to be found on the Sinodun Hills – a pair of small wooded knolls outside Little Whittenham, commonly referred to as the Clumps (or the Bubs, or the Buttocks, depending on who you ask and how drunk they are). The one known as Castle Hill had once been a Roman fort – this is plain to see even in this day and age – and the wisdom was that Centurion gold had been buried there and was waiting to be discovered. Many had tried, especially around an area called, enticingly or perhaps ironically, the Money Pit – but not a groat had ever been found there.

Yet, this wasn't going to put Jack off. A Whittenham man, he had the luck about him. That's what everyone said: 'Born lucky, that Jack!' Things always seemed to go his way, whether it was in the cards, in the courting game, on the sports field or in the field of life.

Having heard about the many failed and foolish attempts to find the Sinodun gold, he decided to try his luck. He had to fair better than those feckless treasure-hunters before him.

And so off he set one misty morning, with a spade on his shoulder, whistling away.

'Where you off to Jack?' called a neighbour.

'I'm off to find that treasure!'

He clomped up to the Clumps, standing lonely in the mist. By the time he got to the top, he was out of puff and stopped to dab his brow at Round Hill. He looked over to the 'Castle', the shadow of the earthworks just visible through the mist. 'Well, no point hanging about,' he said to himself, and he walked across to the other clump. He passed through a tunnel of fairy thorn. Within the enclosure there was a tangle of old trees. With some difficulty, he negotiated the thicket – each snap of twig seeming louder than usual.

Holding his nerve, he continued to the Money Pit, a hollow scooped out of the top of the hill. He walked around it, sizing it up, letting his feet test the ground. Evidence of previous excavations were clear and it looked as though an army of moles had been at it. He wasn't going to get anywhere here. On a whim he decided to strike out at an angle from the pit, towards a notch in the ramparts where the glow of the morning sun could just be seen.

Halfway along, he stopped his pacing and plunged in his spade. This felt like as good a spot as any and so he began to dig. For a while he put his back into it, and was soon a good foot or two down. He whistled while he worked, to keep himself company – it was a lonely sound in the mist, a gravedigger's whistle.

Suddenly, his spade struck something – something hard – with a dull thud. Heart pounding, he cleared away a handful of earth and could see a metal band of intricate workmanship, part of a strong iron box. With renewed energy he cleared the rest away until he could see the whole chest. A treasure chest!

He had found it – Lucky Jack strikes again!

Blessing his good fortune, Jack pulled the chest free with some difficulty. For a moment he sat on the dewy grass, catching his breath, which escaped in clouds.

There it was before him, as real as the day. It had probably not seen sun for many centuries. Dark and solid in the mist, it was a chip off the block of time.

And then he got up and scratched his head. How was he going to open this? There was a big lock on it but it looked rather rusty. Ever the practical man, Jack decided to thwack it one – that usually worked. And so he picked up his spade and was about to strike it when suddenly the silence of the Clumps was shattered by an eerie cronking.

There was a flurry of dark wings, and a huge raven landed on the chest. It looked at Jack with black beady eyes, glinting with intelligence. For an uncomfortable pause, they looked at each other and Jack wondered what was going to happen next. His throat was suddenly in need of a 'wetting'.

To Jack's astonishment, the bird began to speak in a hoarse voice: '*He has not been born yet!*' The raven's voice riveted Jack to the spot, and made him drop the spade. Croaking loudly, the raven took off, circling overhead.

Pale and trembling, Jack acted without thinking – from some primal place of terror. He lowered the chest back into the hole and quickly covered it with earth, stamping it down, stamping it down good, all the while terrified the raven would come back, would speak, with *that* voice.

Jack covered the pit with a large log so that no one would know it had been recently dug.

He picked up his spade and hot-footed it back down the hill, back to the village. He kept going, all the way to The Plough at Long Wittenham. He was in need of a drink of something strong!

The banging on the door eventually stirred the landlord, who knew Jack well – he was a good customer – and so he agreed to let him in early: he could see he had had a 'turn'. Pale as a ghost he was!

Later, tucked quietly by himself in the inglenook, where he hogged the fire to take the chill out of his bones, Jack pondered on what the raven had meant. *He has not been born yet...* Who has not been born yet? The one destined for the treasure? If not him, then who? Perhaps his son ... No, not that good-for-nothing layabout! What about a grandson? Or granddaughter for that matter? Not born yet, but the stork would bring them sooner or later if his son kept sowing his oats like he did!

Maybe one day, Jack reflected, one of his descendants would strike lucky. He sank the rest of his pint, happy with this conclusion. Perhaps, sometimes, you have to pass on the luck.

The appearance of the raven is surprising – it is more associated with Norse or Celtic mythology than Roman. Odin had two ravens – Hugin and Munin ('thought' and 'memory'). Bran the Blessed is associated with the raven – his head is said to been buried at the Tower of London, until dug up by King Arthur – and yet his ravens can be seen there to this day. It is said if they were to leave, the kingdom would fall, and so their wings are clipped just to be on the safe side. Nowadays, the Tower of London is best known for housing the Crown Jewels. Could the presence of the raven at Sinodun suggest another hoard fit for a monarch? When I visited it, I saw a pair of them, circling over Castle Hill. 'He has not been born yet' is tantalising – perhaps a treasure trove will be discovered by a modern day archaeologist or metal-detector enthusiast (no doubt this is why the 'Money Pit' is fenced off). I would prefer

to think of the 'gold' metaphorically, that the kingly potential is within all of us, waiting to awaken: an inner sun.

The Whittenham Clumps (the collective name of Round Hill and Castle Hill) has also been referred to as the Berkshire Bubs (when the landmark formerly resided in that county before the boundary change); and Mother Dunch's Buttocks – a name which refers to a lady of the Dunch family who owned Little Wittenham Manor in the seventeenth century. The Clumps were made famous by the British artist, Paul Nash, who had a special connection with them ('Ever since I remember them the Clumps had meant something to me. I felt their importance long before I knew their history. They were the pyramids of my small world.' Quoted on www.nashclumps.org). The year 2012 marks the centenary of Nash's first paintings of The Clumps. These days, the area is looked after by the Earth Trust, whose centre sits at the foot of the hill. Through their environmental education initiatives they help remind people that the Earth itself is the greatest treasure we have, and we all have to 'pass on the luck' as stewards of the planet, considering future generations in our actions.

Six

ON HOLY GROUND – THE ROLLRIGHT STONES

Old things can be stubborn. People can be like that – and places too. The Rollright Stones are one such place, or should I say three (there's something about this place that makes it hard to count). On the borderlands between Warwickshire and Oxfordshire, high up on a misty, rain-lashed ridge, a lonely traveller wondering if he'd taken the wrong turn – caught in that unsettling uncertainty of direction – would suddenly glimpse clusters of dark figures. Out of the mist they emerge, like characters from an ancient drama: the King's Stone, the King's Men, the Whispering Knights – wizened standing stones, menhir pock-marked with time, yet weathering the ages and the will of men with a deep toughness.

There is always one who thinks he is tougher, who thinks he can ignore the ancient codes that generations have heeded. The Rollrights have long been thought to be a rum place – the haunt of witches. Around such places, superstitions stick. Watch out if you're passing when the church clock of nearby Long Compton strikes midnight – the King's Men come alive, so they say! And on certain saints' days – unspecified to keep you on your toes – both the King and his men come to life. Yet, what is bane to one is boon to another. On Midsummer's Eve, village maids would sneak to the Whispering Knights and place a delicate maiden ear to the rough stone, hoping to hear whispers of their future and fate.

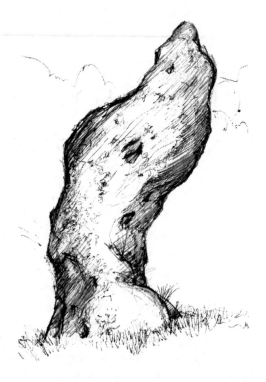

Try and count the stones of the King's Men and you'll get a different tally each time, but be reassured by that – for if you count the same, ill luck is sure to follow. A wily baker once reckoned that he could count the stones by baking a bun for each stone and then laying them out upon the stones. He did not count on the fairies eating them between times, so he failed too. Better not to touch them at all – to touch the King's Men is considered ill luck.

But there was once a farmer who took no heed to such 'foolish stories', and was determined to carry off one of the large stones from the Whispering Knights. He was building an outhouse in his farmyard and he'd had his eye on a particularly fine piece of ancient masonry for just the purpose. His neighbours warned him about such an undertaking, but he paid them no heed. Once he'd set his mind on something, that was that – as stubborn as old Jenny the donkey he was. One morning he woke up, rubbed his hands together and decided, 'Today's the day I'm carrying one of them witch stones away.' He put four horses to his sturdiest waggon and set off up the hill. With a lot of grunting and cursing, he managed to get one of the stones into his waggon.

The sky didn't fall in.

Once he caught his breath, he started to lead his waggon back down the hill, laughing at those foolish stories. But halfway down, his waggon broke in two, and all his horses died at the strain of dragging it back to his farm.

He finally got it to his farmyard, but at what cost? Had it been worth the loss of his waggon and horses? Well, if it showed that nothing would stop him once he set his mind, then yes! He raised the stone in place, and it looked very impressive on the corner of his new outhouse, but from that moment on nothing went right for him – his crops failed, his cattle died – until he was forced to mortgage his land and sell off his remaining horses and waggon; all he had left was a rickety old cart and an old nag who'd seen better days.

Then the penny finally dropped – all his misfortunes had started when he'd brought home that stone. He was determined to right the wrong and set to removing the stone. He placed it in the cart and hitched his old horse to it, but you know what? She pulled it up that hill like it was a pile of hay.

Soon enough, the cart was by the Whispering Knights and the farmer replaced it with his fellows, with a lot less sweating and cursing than before. He felt a huge sense of relief and rode home as light as can be, singing all the way. From then on, his fortunes changed and he prospered, reclaiming all his former wealth and gaining more, but the greatest wealth was the lesson learnt. From that day forth he respected those old witch stones on the top of the misty ridge and always made sure he rolled right with things, and not against.

So, the farmer learnt the hard way, but how did the stones come to be there in the first place? Well, there are as many theories as fairies, but the local wisdom is always the best. A local tale warns of the downfall of another wilful man. It goes like this…

* * *

There was once a strong-minded king, set on invading the rich lands of England with his men. He had got as far as the high windswept ridge on the cusp of the Cotswolds when he was stopped by a wise woman (maybe Mother Shipton herself – certainly by the length of the hairs on her warts you could tell she was a venerable witch indeed). Witches were a common sight around Long Compton. The locals would often say, 'There are enough witches in Long Compton to drag a load of hay up Long Compton Hill.' Be that as it may, the King was not so afeared of the hag he saw before him. He haughtily ignored her, and as he went to stride by, said, 'Out of my way, old woman!' Knowing his mind, the crone challenged him, saying:

'Seven long strides shalt thou take, and
If Long Compton thou canst see
King of England thou shalt be.'

The King laughed at this – seven strides and he'll be king? Lead on! His men seemed reluctant at first, muttering amongst themselves, but a sword is a good persuader. He and most of his men strode confidently forward, but as they approached the top of the hill a great mound grew in front of them, obscuring their view. The witch cackled her cantrip:

'As Long Compton thou canst see
King of England thou shalt not be.
Rise up stick, and stand still stone,
For King of England thou shalt be none,
Thou and thy men hoar stones shall be
And I myself an elden tree.'

The witch raised her bony finger and in a flash, the King and his men were turned to stone. The proud king stood alone, almost on the crest of the hill, waiting forever for his reluctant troops who linger on the opposite side of the road – a circle of stone.

Yet such mighty magic comes at a price. Feeling her old bones stiffen, her skin become even more bark-like than normal, the witch hastened away to her own doom and bumped into four of the King's knights, who had lagged behind and were whispering plots against the King. Peevishly, she turned them to stone as well, and today they are called the Whispering Knights.

This was her final act of witchery – the last drops of her magic leaked from her as she hardened into an elder tree, rooted to the ground.

And there they have stood for a long, long time – King, Knights, King's Men and Crone – seeing wilful men and wise women come and go. A hard lesson in pride; yet few are willing to learn it.

In 1859, it was recorded that folk from Wales took chippings from the Stones to 'keep the Devil off'. A man was offered one pound for a fragment at Faringdon Fair. The beleaguered King's Stone was fenced off between the two world wars, as conscripted troops would chip a slice of stone away to carry with them. Legend has it that this gave them protection in battle.

Yet despite such vandalism, the stones remain, weathering the ages. Now folk come from far and wide to marvel at them, measure and dowse, worship and make strange sounds. But local folk, who know best, see them as special in their own 'simple way'. One day, at the turn of the old century, a folklorist called Arthur Evans reported that one of his informants, a local landowner, met one of his labourers on Good Friday: 'Where do you think I be going?' the man asked, before continuing, 'Why I be agoing to the King-stones, for there I shall be on holy ground.'

The ancient Rollright Stones are a magical place, high upon a ridge overlooking the Cotswolds – a lonely, eerie site. Like iron filings to a magnet, it has attracted stories. The rich combination of folklore was easy to weave into a tale. I have visited it many times over the years – celebrating the turning of the wheel either alone or in a group. I recommend making pilgrimage to it (for it is a sacred site) at different times of year and at different times of day, to get the full effect of this remarkable sacred landscape. Spend time not only amongst the

impressive ring of the King's Men; but also with the twisted menhir of the King's Stone – like a frozen figure striding forth – and with the Whispering Knights, down in the far corner of the field by themselves, where it was said local girls would go to hear the name of their future sweetheart whispered. Once, I sat inside this ancient burial chamber and felt myself being dragged back through the millennia. It was with some effort that I returned to the 'present day'. These stones have their own gravity. Standing quietly by themselves just off the obscure back road, their modest presence has a magic with roots that go deep into the land.

Seven

GEOFFREY THE
STORYTELLER

The stooped, robed man with the whitening beard had been a familiar figure around the castle at Oxenford these last twenty-two years – so much so that nobody noticed as he slipped out a side gate and made his way, as quickly as his robes would allow, along the side of St George's College. It had been his home for over two decades but on the morrow all this was about to change. The air was bitter and his breath came in white clouds. The snow beneath his feet was melting away in pockets, and the patches of grass that were revealed seemed to be the only colour in the wintry landscape.

Yet there, at the edge of the trees, was a sign to gladden his heart: snowdrops. Geoffrey bent to examine them, the first omen of Spring; so frail, yet so tough, to withstand the frosts, the biting winds, and the late snow.

He couldn't remember the last time he had been truly warm.

The scriptorium was draughty and after two decades of scratching away on vellum with a goose feather quill, his hands complained – the cold got into his bones and made them ache. His one true pleasure was agony: writing.

How he loved to daydream and wander into other worlds. Some called it escapism – fanciful make-believe – but Geoffrey

knew there was real value in reverie. All the facts he had read, the dusty dates, the places, the names, the long lineages, swirled around in his head like a flurry of snowflakes, until finally settling onto the blank parchment – his neat Latin script like crow feet in the snow; or the ancient runes and Ogham he had glimpsed. The fact he could read the heathen script he kept to himself. The old stones were fascinating, but were meant to be shunned by the likes of him.

A secular canon for twenty years – tomorrow he would be made a Bishop! The dedication in his last book had paid off to his old colleague Robert De Chesney, the new Bishop of Lincoln. Tomorrow, he would go to Lambeth Palace and be consecrated by Archbishop Theobald for 'good service to his Norman masters'. Geoffrey suspected his consecration was more expedient than anything – as speaker of the old Brythonic tongue, he was probably chosen in an attempt to make the diocesan administration more acceptable in an age when Normans were not at all popular in the areas of Wales which they controlled. Owen Glendower's rebellion was in full swing and he didn't hold out his chances of succeeding in his role.

Yet secretly Geoffrey thrilled at the reports he heard of the rebel king's rise to fame – it felt as though his stories had come true. His fellow countrymen – for was he not one of the Waleas, the 'strangers'? (an ironic name for the indigenous inhabitants usurped by the invaders) – had taken to heart his History of the Kings of Britain – *Historia regum Britanniae* – his magnum opus penned thirteen years before. The stories of the Pendragon had most of all caught the imagination of all who read them and had made his name, so that folk now called him Galfridus Arturus. His own people would call him Geoffrey ab Arthur, which he preferred even more. Son of Arthur! Yet were not all British men 'sons of Arthur', and was not the story he told 'the Matter of Britain'? It was the very soul of the land. When he thought about it, it stirred something within him. As he walked among the trees, he felt it beneath his feet as they crunched into the rigid mulch; in the freezing air; in the tinkling of an icy stream; in the caw of the rooks.

He thought he heard a whisper from the woods. He stopped and scanned the trees. Nothing. His imagination getting the better of him, again! He let out a wisp of breath; turned to continue – then nearly had his heart stopped as a roebuck bounded across his path. For a moment they were eye-to-eye, and Geoffrey caught a glimpse of his own silhouette in the buck's dark orbs. It had seven tines upon each antler. Quickly, it disappeared back into the trees.

Geoffrey lent against a birch tree to catch his breath. His body shuddered into a bellow of laughter. It was good to laugh again – life in the castle was getting very serious of late. The endless Machiavellian machinations were exhausting: the infighting and back-biting; the jockeying for power, for favour, for influence.

Composed at last, he carried on along a small track he knew well enough to find, even when it was covered with a fresh fall of snow.

He had walked here many times over the years to get some fresh air when life in the castle became stifling; to stretch his legs after sitting for too long, hunched over his desk, and to visit an old friend: Myrddin. Strictly speaking (and Merlin was a stickler for detail) that should be Myrddin Silvestris – Merlin of the Woods.

He stepped into the grove and there he was – the 'ancient book' he came to consult. The ghost of a smile played upon his lips. They would never guess this was his primary source!

Geoffrey stood before an ancient oak tree bulging with age. Only two of its main limbs remained, which grew either side of the hollow trunk like antlers. Here was truly the Rex Nemorensis – King of the Grove.

He would sit here, feeling his vertebrae against the ridges of the trunk, for hours, lost in thought. Sometimes he would climb inside and feel a part of the tree, especially when he nodded off and dreamt strange dreams. That's when the whispers would come. It was here, a couple of years ago, that he received the 'life of Merlin'. And twenty years ago, on a day he would never forget, he had first stumbled upon the tree and, in a burst of boyish excitement, tried to climb inside, slipped and banged his head. He ended up upside, his foot caught in the crack, the very image of the Hanged Man, as in those strange cards he had seen once when they were passed amongst the ladies of the court, smiling with amused curiosity at the figures and situations they recognised in each image. Here, hanging for a timeless time, he received the vision. The prophecies came to him then in a flash, the whole lot. For several days after, he hardly slept or ate at all as he feverishly recorded all that he could remember. Half of it didn't seem to make sense, but he simply tried to transcribe rather than interpret.

Prophecies were popular at the time – they always are in uncertain times – and the book was published, copies going to the libraries of the rich. With this success under his belt, he was encouraged to write another. Geoffrey was at first bereft of inspiration for he could not say where such 'voices' came from. He had no more control over them than an epileptic does with his fits.

Then he remembered Myrddin and returned to the tree. This time, he was careful with his footing and managed, after some trial and error, to find a way to 'hear' the voice of the oak. Adopting a more methodical – and less hazardous – approach, he managed to note down the lineage he received, relating right back to Brutus. Every day he would return to the castle with a new scroll of beech bark upon which he had scribbled in Brythonic the words of the wizard. Then, in the scriptorium, he would set about translating them into polished Latin. The wealthy and powerful like to read about … the wealthy and powerful. When he had finished his 'histories' he dedicated it to Robert, Earl of Gloucester and Lord of Glamorgan – who was also the natural son of Henry I and a contender for the throne; Bishop Alexander of Lincoln, Waleran Count of Mellent; and King Stephen. It was a shrewd move that paid off. He had learnt in his time at court that flattery gets you everywhere.

Tomorrow, he would be made a Bishop – but whether it was a blessing or a curse he could not say. St Asaph's was a tainted chalice, an obscure bishopric in the middle of nowhere. Perhaps they just wanted him out of the way. He wouldn't miss the castle, or any of its inhabitants, whom Geoffrey had grown weary with.

Only his friend.

On this day, sacred to Saint Brighid, the festival the pagans call Imbolc, Geoffrey came to say farewell to Myrddin. The tree brooded darkly over him in the white wood. Emotion choked him, so that all he could utter was a terse, 'Thank you'. He placed the rolled-up scroll, covered in wax to protect it from the damp, inside a slot in the tree's split bough; then, laying his hand softly upon the rough bark one last time, he turned and walked away into the snow.

Geoffrey of Monmouth's influence looms large in both early English literature and the oral tradition. He was a consummate storyteller who took obscure sources and wove them into a tantalising tale of Britain's legendary past. He told the rulers of the land what they wanted to know – that they were descended from a long line of kings stretching back to Brutus himself, descended from Aeneas. Apparently landing in Totnes in Devon, Brutus brought 'civilisation' to these 'endarkened isles', lost in the mire of the Dark Ages. He is stated as founding New Troy, or Trinovantum – modern London. The book Geoffrey cites as his source no one has ever identified.

Eight

THE
THREE PLAGUES

King Lludd had three brothers, but the one he loved best of all was Llevelys. Whereas Lludd was mighty in battle, Llevelys was mighty in wit and cunning. They were as thick as thieves together, until Llevelys took for a wife the daughter of the King of France, and crossed the Channel to rule there.

Then calamity struck. There fell upon the isle of Britain Three Plagues, the likes of which were never seen before.

The First Plague was this: a race called the Corannyeid infested the land, and they were able to hear the lightest whisper on the wind, so no one could plot against them.

The Second Plague was this: every May Eve a great scream went up, heard across the land – so terrible it was that it turned men's hair white and weakened their sword-arms; it caused women to miscarry; children to go wild; and livestock, crops and trees to become barren.

The Third Plague was this: however much was held within the King's stores, the fat of the land gathered from the tithe barns of Britain was gone after one night.

The people were desperate. Things could not continue like this!

Lludd consulted his council, and they advised him to consult his brother, the King of France, who was renowned for his wisdom. Yet where could they meet where they would not be heard? Lludd had an idea. He set sail across the English Channel and arranged to meet his brother half-way. Their ships met and the brothers embraced. Before they discussed their plans, Llevelys had a long bronze horn made and they spoke through this, but whatever was said came out the contrary. Wisdom became folly; love became hate. Llevelys perceived there was a devil frustrating them and knew what to do. A good, strong wine was poured through the horn to flush the devil out, so only truth could be heard. *In vino veritas* indeed!

Now they could plan without hindrance. Llevelys had heard of the Three Plagues and knew what to do.

'First take these insects and let them breed; then mash them together with water. Then summon together the Corannyeid and all the people of his realm under the pretence of making peace with them. Then you must scatter the water over the whole crowd and this will drive the enemy out but leave your own people unhurt.'

Then Llevelys explained the cause of the Second Plague: 'The terrible scream is caused by two dragons fighting one another – a native and an invader: red, the British; Saxon, the white. Here is how you remedy it. Measure the length and breadth of the land and where you measure the exact centre dig a pit, fill it with mead, cover it with silk, and wait. The scent of the mead will draw the dragons out. Changing shape, they will fight over it until they grow exhausted, turn into two pigs, then they'll fall into the mead pit, drink the mead and fall asleep. Wrap the pigs in the silk, place them in a stone chest and bury them in the strongest place on the island. As long as they remain there no plague shall befall Britain.'

'As for the Third Plague – it is caused by a mighty magician, who places everyone under a sleeping spell and carries off the food and drink. Place a vat of cold water close by and if you grow sleepy step into the vat. This will keep you awake long enough to catch your culprit.'

Lludd thanked his wise brother and set off back to Britain to heal his kingdom of these Plagues.

Without wasting time he summoned all of his people and the Corannyeid together to broker peace. Meanwhile, he mashed the insects up, mixed them with water, and hid the contents. When everyone had gathered he threw the contents over the entire assembly. As it hit the Corannyeid, they squealed in pain for the mixture was poisonous to them. They fled. And his people were left unharmed. Result!

Next, he set about measuring the length and breadth of the land and he found the exact centre to be Oxford. Here, he had a pit dug and filled it with his finest mead. A piece of silk covered it. And the trap was set. Then the red and white dragons appeared, changing shape in a furious battle until, exhausted, they turned into pigs and plummeted into the mead-pit. There, they drank themselves to sleep. The sound of dragons snoring is a terrible thing! Lludd quickly gathered them up in the silk and placed them in a stone chest. Without sparing the horses, they were taken to the strongest place on the island, under Eyri in the north of Wales, Dinas Emrys, where they were buried. And there they remained, safe and sound.

Finally, Lludd ordered a great feast to be prepared and a vat of cold water placed next to it – he himself standing guard, armed with weapons. There was much feasting and fine entertainment and come the third watch of the night he grew drowsy, but he immersed himself in the icy water, which soon woke him up! In the middle of the night, an armoured giant with a basket on his back stole into the hall and starting helping himself to the feast, carrying off all the food and drink. Lludd marvelled that the basket could hold so much. He set off after the feast-thief, crying, 'Stop! Stop!' Lludd challenged him to a fight there and then, shirking not at the giant's size. The giant threw his basket to the ground and set to it. Sparks flew as their weapons clashed, but Lludd overcame his enemy and cast him down. The giant pleaded for his life. Lludd made him vow to make good his losses. The giant not only agreed to this, but also to be his loyal champion from then on.

And so Lludd had succeeded, with the help of his brother, to rid the land of the Three Plagues, and he ruled his kingdom in peace and prosperity for the length of his life. His name lives on – for he founded the city of Caer Lludd, which we know today as London.

And that's a fact!

Although this tale (Lludd and Llevelys) originates in The Mabinogion *– the classic collection of Welsh legends compiled by Lady Charlotte Guest from earlier sources – the prominence of Oxford within it was too important to miss. The 'city of dreaming spires' is often cited as being the centre of England; although my old home town of Northampton would dispute that claim. However, we are happy for Oxford to keep its pit of drunken dragons! A dramatic, brooding hill covered in tangled trees and mossy boulders, Dinas Emrys does seem like the ideal place to bury such beasts and this dovetails into the story of Merlin and Vortigern's tower. The remnants of a structure dating from the sixth century was found upon it, although to date no dragons of any hue have been found there; yet its name preserves its legendary associations: Emrys is a variant of one of Merlin's many epithets – Merlin Ambrosius. Ambrosia was meant to be the food of the gods – and mead comes pretty close (although too much and one can feel like a pig in a coffer!).*

Nine

THE SCHOLAR
AND THE BOAR

On the 26th of December, St Stephen's Day, a strange and ancient custom is held in the hallowed halls of Queen's College, Oxford – the Boar's Head Feast. A stuffed wild boar, orange in its mouth, is brought in with great pomp and ceremony by three chefs followed by a solo singer, accompanied by torch-bearers and a choir. The soloist sings the Boar's Head Carol, dating back to the fifteenth century.

While the verses are sung, the procession stand still; when the chorus is sung they move forward. Finally, the boar is presented on the high table to the Masters of the college. The Provost distributes herbs to the chorus and the orange goes to the soloist. Then the feast begins in earnest! This custom, dating back to the thirteenth century, is held to commemorate a famous anecdote in the history of the college.

A scholar was out walking in Shotover Forest, to the north of Oxford in the region known as Otmoor – a marshland notorious for rum doings. He was deep in philosophical reverie, considering a tome by Aristotle, when he was suddenly assailed by a ferocious wild boar which charged him from the undergrowth, tusks flashing, shrill squeal splitting the air. Thinking on his feet, the scholar thrust the tome in his hands into the boar's mouth, stopping it dead in its tracks, crying out: *'Glaecum est!'* (with compliments of the Greeks). The boar was overcome by this quick-thinking scholar and thus the savage was conquered by the sage.

And so, to commemorate this wild hog story, the Boar's Head Feast is held every St Stephen's Day.

Yet, its origins might date back even further, for in Norse tradition a sacrifice was made at midwinter to Freyr to ask for favour for the coming year. Freyr is known as Ingwi in Saxon, and associated with the rune Ingwaz, the rune of new beginnings, new opportunities and new life; and of peace and harmony – it seemed Peace on Earth and goodwill to all men was something even the Vikings valued at this time of year. In old Swedish art, St Stephen, whose feast day is, as we know, the 26th of December, is depicted tending horses and offering a boar at a Yuletide feast. In Sweden to this day, a fine leg of Christmas ham is a traditional addition to the family feast.

And so, there is a possibility that an ancient midwinter sacrifice to the Norse god Freyr is enacted every year in Queen's College, Oxford – a notion to relish, but perhaps one that is best *ervitor cum sinapio*: served with mustard!

Here are the lyrics to the ancient Boar's Head Carol (one version of several):

The boar's head in hand bear I
Bedecked with bay and rosemary
I pray you, my masters, be merry
Quot estis in convivio.
(However many are at the feast)

Chorus:
Caput apri defero,
Reddens laudes domino.
(I bring the boar's head,
giving praises to the Lord)

The boar's head, as I understand,
Is the rarest dish in all this land,
Which thus bedecked with a gay garland
Let us *servire cantico*
(serve with song)

Chorus

Our steward hath provided this
In honor of the King of bliss
Which, on this day to be served is
In *Reginensi atrio*
(in the Queen's hall)

Chorus

Ten

THE
DRAGON CUP

The two armies lined up either side of the ice-cold river Brue; the banners of the white horse of Wessex and the black hound of Mercia faced each other above the arrow-heads of tents. They had been camped there, on the flood meadow, for many days. Food and firewood was in short supply and tempers were frayed. It was the dead of winter and it seemed hope had died also. The endless cold was making the men sharp-tongued and quick to violence. The warriors of Beorna were like bears with sore heads, surly and dangerous. They took to sharpening their weapons and polishing their armour.

They had come to Bernecestre to make a treaty – for it stood on the borderland between Mercia and Wessex. Two kingdoms at war, and caught in the middle – Beorna, the local chieftain, who gave his name to 'the fort of the warriors of the Bear'. He had protected his people for many seasons; his great beard was peppered, his heavy brows bearing a slash of white scar across one side. He wore the bearskin of his totem – the mighty fur draped over his massive frame and covering his crown with a frozen snarl. He leant upon his favourite weapon, the two-handled battle-axe and spat into the mud of the Pingle – the no man's land stretching across to the enemy camp. To step foot on it was an act of war. The armies were

on tenterhooks, and looking for the slightest provocation not to sign the treaty. The peace treaty had taken many months of negotiation, largely by the white-cloaked priests – who prided themselves on being meek, humble peacemakers. At first these strange 'men of the white' were mocked by Beorna and his warriors – they were not *real* men. No steel by their thigh, only twigs, some jibed. Yet something about their humble persistence intrigued Beorna – after knowing decades of conflict he was weary.

Surely, there had to be another way?

In the centre of the Pingle there was a single oak tree. Its branches swirled in the wind, which howled around the armies that day, bringing with it biting hailstones, clattering onto the carts, hissing into the braziers, sending anything not secured flying: stools and tankards, shields and banners. There was a devil in the air, all the men agreed. Beorna growled at them, and his entourage fell silent.

'Are you warriors, or women?' he bellowed. 'I need men today – for what we have to do takes strength and courage. Any fool can make war; but it takes a wise man to make peace.'

'But the Mercians are scum!' snarled one of his shieldmen. More murmurs of assent. 'They have raided our lands for decades, raping our women, stealing our cattle, burning our villages. And you want us to make peace with them!' Roars of indignation echoed around the mead-hall.

'Yes! As the White Brothers say, if we do not forgive, how can we ever move on? How can things heal?'

Sounds of scepticism hissed like rain in the fire-pit.

'It may seem strange to us,' Beorna continued, 'we are more used to letting our steel do the talking.' The men laughed in self-congratulation. 'But for once, men, think with the steel up here.' He clonked his helm with his axe.

* * *

Beorna and his Royal Guard made their way to the ford and crossed the turbid waters to the Pingle, slipping on the muddy bank. They reached the oak at the same time as the iron-eyed Mercians. They eyed each other warily. In the shelter of the tree a table had been set up with scrolls, ink, quills and hot wax for sealing. On the table sat the Dragon Cup, used for oath-making for generations; it was an ancient wooden goblet that 'once belonged to a great king.' A serpent wound around its base, carved in exquisite detail, eating its own tail, wings extending to the chipped gold rim, worn smooth with the mouths of chieftains and champions who have supped from it, raising a toast to peace.

Testily, the two kings sat looking at each other across the table. The Danish king cast a cold eye over Beorna, the Wessex chieftain. He was renowned for his ferocity, and his 'fort of the warriors of the bear' was the thorn in Mercians side. The constant raiding and skirmishes along the borders was an expensive distraction. Like two wild siblings, Mercia and Wessex fought for the bigger territory, for the lion's share – yet after decades of attrition both kings realised neither was gaining anything from this. It would be of mutual benefit to reach an accord – and that is why they had come, on this cold winter's day. A fire guttered in the corner, the icy wind teasing the flaps of the tent. Around them, stern bodyguards watched on – the elite from both sides.

Before them was the Dragon Cup.

Mercia spoke first. 'You're bear-shirts raid our territories.'

Beorna considered this. 'They merely claim back what is theirs – from lands you stole.'

The air crackled between them and the cup seemed to crack also, or was it just the fire spitting?

'Stole, or won in victory? Surely Beorna acknowledges the right of the victor? This very cup is a spoils of war – it has been handed down through out bloodline for generations, yet here I see it before me.'

The cup cracked a little more.

'Yet whose was it originally, my friend? Did not your ancestors seize it from a royal hoard, plundering the barrows of the dead?'

'Lies! It was a gift from the gods – it was found by a pool one day, left by the Unseen Ones.'

This time the cup cracked in two. Both looked on, astonished. And then there was uproar. The meeting ended in disarray. The kings returned to their armies, where talk of an imminent battle rippled through the ranks. This would be a day not of peace, but of slaughter. There would be plenty for the crows to feed upon, come morning.

* * *

Then, at first light, as mist rose from the frosted ruts of the Pingle, a man in a white robe came, walking boldly between the armies, chanting something caught in snatches on the wind. Was he moon-touched? He walked towards the tent, now unguarded and empty, save for the fragments of the Dragon Cup. He went and emerged with them, holding the shattered shards aloft. Both armies looked on in grim silence. The air was tense. Who was this fool? A battle was about to take place – if he doesn't get out of the way, he will taste steel.

'Brave and mighty Kings of Mercia and Wessex. Brave and mighty warriors – hail and heed!' Though he looked frail, he voice was clear as a mountain stream and carried across both camps, across the frozen land. 'I hold the Dragon Cup – long has this sacred vessel bequeathed sovereignty on its owner, but look at its state. A symbol of this broken land. It is said when three untruths were spoken over it, it shall shatter – and you see the result.'

Warriors from Mercia growled: 'You call our king a liar? We will tear that tongue from your head!'

Unflinching, the priest continued. 'You both lay claim to this place, but who, ultimately, owns this land?' He did not wait for an answer. 'The one true God himself! His Spirit binds all, transcends all. Without it, we shall destroy each other until nothing is left. Only the love of Spirit maintains this Matter, the flesh of the Earth. And we are part of it.' As the priest spoke, the cup started to mend itself. 'Both kings have equal claim, and shall be equal stewards of this land. Long have their people lived here. Who owns the land? Any who work upon it, who worship upon it, who give their loyalty and love it.' The cup mended some more. 'Live together in peace – may you come here to trade goods and tales. Come drink the Dragon Cup and forge the sword of peace.' The final fragment fell into place. The cup was mended. The priest held it aloft, to the gasps and murmurs of those gathered. 'Three untruths break it; three truths mend it. I have spoken, and the spirit of the one true God is through me!'

The two kings came forward, with their royal bodyguards. They took turns to examine the cup and were impressed. The priest poured some wine into the cups 'To Peace.'

Beorna slowly raised it and drank. Looking at his enemy with a level, penetrating gaze, he spoke the words like a challenge, daring him to defy them: 'To Peace.'

Finally, the Mercian king did the same. 'To Peace.'

The Bear-Chieftain addressed both armies. 'A great miracle has been performed here this day. Let a temple be raised on this spot to house your spirit, and this cup. Let it be remembered, so none may forgot its healing magic.'

Time flows on. Kings and knaves turn to dust. But sometimes a trace of their lives remain. Beorna's name endured; the place by the banks of the river Brue became known as the 'fort of the warriors of the Bear' – Bicester – and if you go to the church of St Edburg's you'll see, in two of the windows, the Dragon Cup.

This tale was inspired by the stained-glass windows in the ancient church of St Edburg, two of which depict the 'Dragon Cup'. I used this motif in imagining a kind of 'creation myth' for Bicester, based upon the historical evidence of its earliest inhabitants. Sometimes a 'story of place' is enshrined in a name, when all other evidence has vanished – and so the 'fort of the warriors of the bear', or the 'tribe of the warriors of Beorna', seemed too enticing to turn down. The Pingle can still be seen, demarcating the lovely old town from the 'designer village' which has spawned on Bicester's edge. Different forces besiege the town these days. What would Beorna think of it all?

The motif of the 'four-squared cup of truth' comes from Celtic tradition (I first came across it in John and Caitlin Matthews' Celtic Wisdom Tarot).

Eleven

FRIDESWIDE AND THE TREACLE WELL

Frideswide was renowned for her beauty, but she had hoped to escape the unwanted attention of men when she took the veil – retreating from the world behind the walls of the convent at Oxford.

Alas, this was not to be, for word of her legendary beauty reached the ears of Aelfgar, King of Mercia. The fact she was a nun did not put him off. He set out to behold her beauty himself. He camped outside the convent with his rough and ready army, and waited. It was clear that the slavering bunch of heathens would not restrain themselves for long – not with such rich pickings at hand. Rather than risk bringing ruin upon the convent, Frideswide fled. Scenting the thrill of the hunt, Aelfgar pursued her with renewed vigour – alone – into the wild wood which grew beyond the water meadows.

Heart thudding in her chest, Frideswide darted through the trees like a deer pursued by a pack of hounds; until she found her way blocked by a thickly flowing stream. She cried out in dismay. As her pursuer approached, she fell to her knees to pray.

Aelfgar snorted like a boar, stroking his beard as he approached. He had run his quarry to ground.

'Odin's blood, woman! I am not used to being denied. You gave me a hearty chase, but now – where is my reward?' Suddenly, a blinding pain shot through Aelfgar's eyes and he doubled over in agony. 'Aargh! What witchery is this?' Aelfgar raised his hands before him. The woods, the woods were dark…

The gods deemed fit to punish him in his lusty pursuit, striking him blind! He howled with rage as he stumbled over roots and bumped painfully into branches and trunks.

Rather than take advantage of this stroke of divine luck, Frideswide took pity on the afflicted King and turned back to help him. She prayed to Saint Margaret – and miraculously a spring bubbled up. Frideswide cupped some of the clear water in her hand and bathed the eyes of the King. Suddenly, his sight was restored by this 'treacle'; this healing fluid.

Aelfgar was a changed man – the scales, as they say, fell from his eyes and he saw the error of his ways, renouncing any designs on Frideswide and his heathen faith. The King turned to the God of Christ and Frideswide was allowed to return to her convent, her chastity intact. She dwelled there in peace for the remainder of her days, building a small chapel by the well, which would one day become the present church of the parish.

The legend of Binsey's treacle well grew over the centuries as the dreaming spires of Oxford became a venerable seat of learning. Yet, even in such a place, folly persisted. Waggish Oxford undergraduates would send gullible tourists to search for the village's famous treacle well and treacle mines. At least the former had some credence – it was Frideswide's healing well. The latter could perhaps be imagined to be the nearby shallow ponds in the summer, covered with a thick yellow slime.

The treacle well became neglected through time, its source choked with weeds. This dismal state of affairs continued to the point when, in 1850, a visitor declared that the well had been lost. Local folk claimed to know nothing about it.

Fortunately, in 1857, a local vicar, Reverend Thomas Prout, a don of Christ Church, rediscovered it and restored it by 1874, with a protective archway and stone steps, with a clear inscription dedicating it to St Margaret.

Countless pilgrims have sought it ever since as a cure for eye complaints and other bodily disorders, yet it has also been a source of inspiration – an Oxfordshire Mimir. If this seems fanciful, then consider its mythic status in English literature…

One idyllic afternoon in 1862, the Reverend Charles Lutwidge Dodgson rowed towards Godstow with his friend Robinson Duckworth and three guests – Lorina, Alice and Edith Liddell, the young daughters of the Dean of Christchurch. To pass the time, the girls asked for a story and Dodgson happily obliged, conjuring a tale of three children – Elsie, Lacie and Tillie – who lived at the bottom of the treacle well.

The story so delighted the girls that the Reverend was encouraged to write it down – which he did under his pen name, Lewis Carroll – and *Alice in Wonderland* was born. Frideswide's treacle well became a rabbit hole and its magical properties took on a completely different dimension.

The well has gained an extra significance now, as the inspiration for Lewis Carrol's children's classic. Near the well, within the peaceful churchyard, there is a grave decorated with stone roses dedicated to Mary Ann Prickett. The governess of Dean Liddell's children, she was the inspiration for the Red Queen (nicknamed 'Pricks' by the children). It is a curious coincidence that Thornbury is the old Saxon name for the site.

When I went to visit the famous well, it took some finding – I had to ask directions at the local inn, The Perch. The friendly French barman was very helpful and said that the well was 'very special' and that the best time to see it was during an eclipse, when the water became 'thicker'. Finally locating it, I was delighted by the picturesque setting – a small isolated chapel with a congregation of goats. There was evidence of veneration: withered flowers; a card; and a little fairy statuette. I fished a pen out of the viscous yellowy water, low within its chamber: the ultimate ink-well. Sitting on a wooden seat carved from a stump, I contemplated the 'stickiness' of such places. It is fascinating how one narrative can inspire another, and how this accretion of narrative can draw visitors to a place, and enrich their perception of it, so that it is experienced with a 'mythic filter'.

How many more 'rabbit holes' have been inspired by Lewis? It has become a familiar point of reference in popular culture: for example in the film The Matrix, Neo is asked, 'How far down the rabbit hole do you want to go?'

What would St Frideswide make of it all? From Aelfgar to Alice, the Treacle Well has continued to flow – long may it do so.

Twelve

SPANISH WATER

'The rain in Spain falls mainly on the plain…' Lucy recited this to herself as she made her way, old milk bottle in hand, along with her friends and fellow villagers from Leafield, to the magic spring. The spring had been venerated in Wychwood by the folk of the forest for as long as anyone could remember. A good spirit was said to reside in it – as long as it was kept sweet – which could heal folk of all kinds of ailments: from eye to heart; from back to bowels.

It was Easter Monday, and they were off to make 'Spanish Water'. Lucy, the new girl in the village, felt a bit embarrassed, because everyone seemed to know what this meant except her. When she had asked her friends they had giggled, as though it was obvious and she shouldn't be so foolish.

The bluebells were out and carpeted the floor of the forest either side of the track. The clean Spring sunlight pierced the tangled canopy, budding with new growth. Lucy had always lived in the forest, although only in Leafield for less than year, and found the presence of trees comforting. They seemed to sing to her as she walked to and from school; as she played with her friends; as she sat with her Gran on her porch – they were the constant soundtrack of her life. She knew there was a big wide world out there – she was

quite good at geography and could list the capitals of Europe; even knew a little bit of French and German – but she had never gone beyond Oxford, which had seemed like a teeming metropolis to her when she had visited it with her father once. She had developed neck-ache from looking up so much at the dreaming spires, which seemed to stretch to Heaven. They visited one of the churches, St Giles, and its fluted vaults seemed to mirror a forest grove in stone.

Yet it was in Wychwood that she felt a true presence, though of what exactly she couldn't say. This was her place of worship, where she often felt something – ancient, deep and sacred – in the wood, in the soil, in the stone. It was in her bones. And today she wasn't alone, at least a hundred of the villagers processed to the old well, with their bottles, led by the local priest, Reverend Hartlake. In their Sunday best they made an odd sight walking through the forest in solemn silence. It was like some kind of dream.

They passed Hatching Hill and Maple Hill; the long barrows between Slatepits and Churchill Copse; until they came to the small stone trough, half covered with a thicket and dripping with moss. There, from a little gap, the glittering water trickled out.

The priest stepped onto a stone next to it and the parishioners bowed their heads in prayer. Reverend Hartlake was canny and knew he could not stop the villagers from continuing this questionable tradition, so he had made a point for many years now of coming along with them and giving it his official blessing.

One by one they filled up their bottles, which took some time, but nobody seemed to be in a rush. When Lucy was finished she held the glass bottle up and it seemed to catch the sunlight – until the next in line coughed, and she moved on to make room.

And then, holding their glass, now cool and dappled with droplets, they sang hymns praising the risen Christ. Reverend Hartlake talked about the 'Water of Life' and how it should always be shared. Then the formal part was over and freshly baked Easter biscuits were offered around – folk picnicked in small groups, breaking bread amid the green.

Then Old Bliss the Teller settled down on a stump and told them a strange story, how once in the land travellers were offered refreshing draughts from wells, such as this one they sat next to, by maidens with cups of gold. Until one day a greedy king, Amangons, wanted the cup, the water and the maiden for himself. He took by force what had been given freely. His knights followed suit, despoiling the other maidens and desecrating their wells. Amangons had his cup of gold – but at what cost? He retired to his castle where he became ill – his maiden could not help him. He could not die or get better, but lived on and on, becoming the Fisher King. The land became a wasteland, the wells were abandoned and no traveller was offered a cup of gold any more.

Old Bliss lit his pipe and sat back, contemplating a smoke ring.

'Is that it?' asked Lucy, disappointed by the ending.

'Oh no, young missy! That's not the end of it by a long chalk. Then a young knight came, from a distant land, pure of heart, who, upon hearing about the Fisher King, decided to go and help.

He journeyed to his castle, and, finding it and the King in a terrible state, he set to make things better. Amangons withered away on his throne, coughing and groaning with no one to serve or care for him. The knight felt compassion in his heart. 'Your Majesty, what ails thee?' he asked. The King coughed hoarsely and weakly gestured for a cup. The knight found an old golden goblet, gave it a wipe with the sleeve of his tunic and filled it with good clean water from his own waterskin, before offering it to the King. Amangons stretched out a shaking hand and slowly, painfully, drank it. He immediately felt better, the light returning to his eyes. He looked upon the good knight and smiled, saying: 'The Grail is in the giving; not the taking.' The Fisher King was healed and the land laid waste no more.

Old Bliss concluded his story to a round of applause.

'What about the maidens and the cup of gold?' asked Lucy.

'My, you are a curious one, aren't you!' Laughter rippled around the glade. 'Well, they seemed to vanish from the land, but now and again, if you're lucky, you might catch a glimpse of one, offering a cup of kindness to a passing stranger.' He winked at his audience. 'Which reminds me...' He smacked his lips. 'Anyone have a drink for a thirsty teller?'

Hartlake, who had been listening to the tale with stern attention, suggested to the villagers they must share the Waters of Life, otherwise they might turn corrupt too! Scowling fondly at Old Bliss, the Reverend declared to his flock it was time to return. The villagers followed, and someone struck up a tune on a fiddle. An Easter Monday fair awaited them upon their return, tables laid out with fine food and drink. They had completed their rite of Spring and had made 'Spanish Water' – Holy Water.

Lucy savoured her bottle of sunlight, cool in her hands, and stored up the memories of the day: the bluebells; Hartlake's sermon; Old Bliss's tale; and the blessing of the wood – which was the best medicine of all. And you don't need to go to Spain to enjoy that.

This story was inspired by the following fragment, which I found in Katherine Briggs' The Folklore of the Cotswolds:

On Easter Monday the people of Leafield considered it their right to go to one of the forest springs to make 'Spanish Water'. This was kept as a remedy for almost every disorder. On Easter Monday I have met troops of Leafield people going through the forest with their bottles to make Spanish Water.

Another source, June Lewis-Jones' Folklore of the Cotswolds, says this was done on Palm Sunday: 'The reputedly miraculous spring water of Wychwood was mixed with Spanish liquorice and lemon to make a cure-all to last the entire year.' Holy Water was deemed to be rainwater caught on Holy Days, such as Easter and the many saints' days. This was particularly prized for bathing sore eyes in, as it was water which 'ran against the sun', that is from west to east. Other Spring customs persisted in the Wychwood area, suggesting that this was once a common folk practice – perhaps a remnant of the worship of water by the Celts.

Thirteen

A Gift
of Water

The gift of life flows and should never be owned. Water is a miracle that makes life on Earth possible. It is a precious resource that links us all — without it we would perish. A clean glass of water is the same to a thirsty man, whatever nationality he is. Wherever on Earth we dwell, this universal water table connects us all; yet sometimes it wells up in unexpected places...

A village in the Chilterns is perhaps the last place you would expect to see a Maharajah's well. To a thirsty traveller walking the Icknield Way – that ancient trackway running a couple of miles by Ipsden, as it was then – the well might appear like a mirage, yet it is real, found within the parish of Stoke Row. Sitting within its own small park, complete with a small cottage, it is a most splendid edifice – an onion-shaped dome covering the well-head, where winch apparatus is protected by a golden elephant like some Indian shrine. How did it come about?

It was the mid-nineteenth century and the Empire was in full swing. Half the world was painted pink and an Ipsden man was doing his bit for HIM (Her Imperial Majesty). Mr Edward Reade, the local squire, had worked with the Maharajah of Benares in India for many years. One of his many deeds there was to sink a

well in 1831, to aid a local community in Azimurgh. He talked about how water was often a problem for villagers in his homeland – the chalk hills of the Chilterns – after a dry spell.

When Mr Reade finally left the area in 1860, he asked the Maharajah to ensure that the well remained available to the public.

A couple of years later, the Maharajah decided on an endowment in England. He recalled Mr Reade's generosity in 1831 and also remembered his stories of water deprivation in his home area of Ipsden. It was surprising to hear of this: a drought … in England? And yet it made the seat of the Empire more human and endearing. Perhaps these 'white lords' weren't invulnerable after all. The Maharajah's compassion was piqued. And so the well in Stoke Row, as Ipsden became known, duly came about.

It was dug, by hand, all three hundred and sixty-eight feet of it, to a width of four feet. Greater than the height of St Paul's

Cathedral; more than twice the height of Nelson's Column. It took about a year to build. Hard work, backbreaking work – yet it created local employment nonetheless.

The well and superstructure cost a princely sum of £353 13s 7d. The elephant and machinery cost a further £39 10s, the project was undertaken by the local firm of Wilder in Wallingford, still to be found in the town. Finally, a cottage was raised for the modest cost of £74 14s 6d. This was where the well-keeper would dwell, to maintain the Maharajah's gift.

The well was opened officially on Queen Victoria's birthday in 1864. The winch turned and the water flowed – a miracle from below!

The well remained in use for over seventy years – a lifetime – until pipes brought water to the village from reservoirs, and cottages started to acquire rudimentary plumbing. After that, it was used less and less, but has been preserved as a symbol of a special friendship spanning continents.

Wherever you live in the world, water is precious. Perhaps the Maharajah's Well in Stoke Croft will help remind us of that, thanks to this noble gift.

Links with the Maharajah continue to the present day. When Queen Elizabeth II was visiting Benares (these days known as Varanasi) in 1961, the Maharajah pointed out that the well was shortly coming up to its centenary. He invited the Duke of Edinburgh to visit Stoke Row for the celebrations. This he duly did, arriving in his red helicopter – a detail preserved in the village newspaper, adorning the logo. A little corner of Oxfordshire is connected, through this remarkable monument, to the blue blood of two continents.

Fourteen

THE SNOW
FORESTERS

There's an old saying: 'Stow on the Wold, where the wind blows cold and the cooks have nothing to cook.' And cold and hungry they were, those poor tinkers passing through the ghost-webbed groves of Wychwood that night. It was Christmas Eve and they were making their way across the 'Wolds from Burford to Stow. The gypsies, road-hardened as they were, were having a hard time of it – for it was blowing a blizzard and their best nag, Old Ness, struggled to pull their barrel-top caravan up the steep snow-bound lane towards the hill-top town. They were passing through a lonely stretch of road that ran by a wood outside Idbury – it was shunned by travelling folk for being haunted by the Snow Foresters – the un-peaceful dead. Can you not hear them screeching and scratching on the caravan window with their icy fingers? Inside, the family huddled together and out front Pa gritted his teeth and tugged on the reins harder. They had to find shelter, and soon!

The snow howled around them outside, as though it was alive with a malign intelligence, seeking out every gap. Their teeth chattered and their knees knocked together.

'If Old Ness don't hurry up, the Snow Foresters'll get us,' they wailed.

Suddenly, they heard another sound at the door – the boy heard it first. 'There's something out there!'

'Sshhh, lad.'

'No, listen – it's a mewing! It's a kit-cat. We can't leave it out in the cold!' He opened the door and a little white kitten came in, shivering, snowflakes melting on its fur.

'Put it out!' said the mother, for they believed such creatures were a death-token.

'No Mam, it's as lost as us and as little as me. Us can't turn it out. Is it not Christmas Eve?'

'Tis so,' replied his Mam.

'Then will speak to us, if we ask it in rhyme: Is it, Kit-Cat?'

The kitten replied, 'Tis so!'

The family gasped.

Having their attention, it continued: 'And you'll all win safe through if ye can keep on to the church bells. Hearken to the birds a-twittering and follow after them – for they go to join in the carols at Stow.'

Well, when a cat speaks, even a little one, it's worth listening to, and so this is what the family did.

'Listen!' said the son, who had ears keener than the rest.

Above the howling, the scritch-scratching and the tap-tapping, the gypsy family heard the sound of hundreds of little birds flying by.

The sound warmed their hearts, and gave them courage and a new strength to carry on – Old Ness ploughed on through the snow and they sung carols to keep their spirits up and keep the Snow Foresters at bay.

Finally, they came to lodge on the outskirts of Stow, and there a kindly farmer let them in for the night, for the sake of Christmas charity: and not a moment too soon. They were chilled to the bone but were soon thawing out around a cosy fire with something warming in a glass. They toasted the turning of the wheel of fortune. It had just passed the stroke of midnight, the Christmas bells were ringing and the snow had finally stopped, and the little white kit-cat was gone.

The little lad said. 'I knew it! She wasn't a witch's cat. I think, I think … she was a little fallen angel that was earning her way back to Heaven.'

'Ah,' said Granny, thawing out by the fire. 'Then that was another good deed for her.'

And the family thought on as they fell asleep, huddled cosily together by the hearth, what good deeds they had done that year to help them find their way back to the hearth of Heaven.

Perhaps they were all a little closer.

This heart-warming tale straddles the border with Gloucestershire and also appears in Anthony Nanson's folk tales of that county. He tells it in his own style, as no doubt fellow storytellers from neighbouring villagers would do, sharing the mythology of the region.

A gypsy horse fair still takes place in Stow, and the odd barrel-top caravan can occasionally be seen parked up on the Fosseway, offering fortune telling. Whether the white kit-cat or the Snow Foresters have been seen or heard again, both locals and travellers keep mum.

Fifteen

THE
WHITE HARE

Will, Jack and Lewis were inseparable friends. They lived in Long
Compton and went everywhere together. One night, they were out
netting rabbits by Barton's Grove. It was a full moon and it shone
through the trees like a lantern, casting everything in silver and
black. They ribbed each other about the many tales of witches who
lived in the area; 'There are enough witches in Long Compton to

draw a load of hay up Long Compton Hill,' they would cackle, trying to make each other scared, but they laughed it off – until they caught sight of a white hare. There. There it was! But as soon as it was pointed out, it dashed behind a hedge. Had they been seeing things? But then, there it was again – running in a circle by a gate. As they carried on, the hare seemed to be running in decreasing circles around them.

This unsettled them a little, though none of them wanted to admit it. They weren't having much luck catching rabbits and now that the moon had set, it seemed very dark.

'Shall we go back?' suggested one and they all nodded, relieved somebody had said it. They slung their guns over their shoulders and started to head homewards.

While they followed the path home, which their feet knew well enough to find the way in the dark, they sensed movement behind them. They froze. At first, they did not want to turn, but then one by one they looked and there was the white hare. Whenever they moved, it moved too, clinging to them like a white shadow.

'Run!'

As one they bolted, but the hare was fast.

They pegged it across Duffus Close, until they came to a cottage of one of them. They leapt across the garden wall into the back garden. The key was found under the pot but the boy struggled to make it fit the lock, he was shaking so. Just as the door was forced open and the three fell in, collapsing in a heap, they saw the white hare sitting on the garden wall. It watched them with its moon-mad eyes. Caught in its glare, the lads found themselves frozen to the spot as they heard a voice inside their heads telling them a chilling story:

I had always led a simple life, in harmony with the land, harming none – indeed folk would often come to me with their ailments and woes, just as often for a listening ear as a charm or potion. My herbal remedies were highly regarded in the district. No one knew more about the plants and secret ways of nature than Old Nan of

Long Compton. They said I was as old as the hills, but though I had seen eight decades I wasn't quite that ancient!

Then one September night, a local labourer, James, was returning home from the fields after having more than his share of the green wage – cider – mixed with a gallon of beer. Purely medicinal was his excuse, having recently been suffering from pains, cramps and swollen legs. He was cursing the air black and blue, blaming his aches upon the witches of Long Compton.

Well, that's not a wise thing to curse in our neighbourhood, or any. An old lady overheard him and came out to ask him to quieten down. 'What was all the commotion about, young James?' James got uppity and saw me – for it was I, Old Nan, who had known him since he was a lad – as the chief cause of his woes. Losing his temper James slashed me over the head with his sickle, to 'draw the blood above the breath', as fools said, thinking that was the way to destroy a witch's power. Well, his drunken blow hit home harder than perhaps he'd liked and poor Old Nan fell down dead.

And that is how folk found me – and James – who stuck by his madness that I'd been a witch who had harmed him. He made up some foolish tale about me preventing him from working with my art, though for what reason, he could not say. And worse, there were sixteen witches like that in the area who should be treated just the same. He was placed in the local jail until he sobered up and was then brought to justice, standing trial for my murder. In the dock, he stood sullen and silent. On his behalf, the barrister said he had acted in self-defence, believing himself to be under attack from the witches of Long Compton.

Hares have long ears, and a very pale one eavesdropped upon James' discussion with the superintendent, hearing him say the water thereabouts was 'full of witches' and would get inside him. He cited the death of horses and cattle – he had seen them wither away before his eyes – who had fallen under the influence of the Evil Eye. Incredibly, he was not alone in these opinions; some of his neighbours shared his delusion. And the judge decided he would not hang for his crimes, because of his insanity. Instead, he would be detained at Her Majesty's pleasure. Even in prison he did not feel safe from us witches – so powerful we must be! He refused to eat and drink and weakened away, and in his lonely cell he died.

Yet his deed was remembered – how James the labourer had cruelly killed an innocent old lady. Poor Old Nan! Such deeds are not forgotten. They live on after us. And since that time a white hare has been seen, especially on moon-kissed nights.

Remember Old Nan's tale, and be kind to the elderly, young 'uns – and mind what you go a-hunting on a full moon.

The voice stopped, the white hare blinked, and hopped back into the shadows.

From then on, Will, Jack and Lewis gave up hunting rabbits, hares, or anything with long-ears for that matter, and were very kind to the elders of the village!

This tale straddles the border between Oxfordshire and Warwickshire – the lads stray over 'the other side', both geographically and metaphorically. There is a neat folkloric 'wildlife corridor' with the Rollright Stones story, which mentions Long Compton. It was commonly believed that a Hares' Parliament took place in Oxfordshire – where the hares stand facing each other in a circle like witches at a sabbat. I suspect Old Nan would have been a member.

Sixteen

THE HIGHWAYMEN OF WYCHWOOD FOREST

Tom, Dick and Harry Dunsdon were bad lads. Perhaps it was where they lived – for Wychwood Forest was a notorious haunt for ne'er-do-wells. It seemed to have more than its fair share of maggoty apples – poachers, cut-purses, robbers, and cock-fighters. And yet the Dunsdons came from a respectable yeoman family at Fulbrook.

Perhaps it was simply boyish bravado, a bad influence, or a chance opportunity, but whatever made them break the law, they went from bad to worse. They moved to a little cottage at Icomb which had an underground passage to a cave, screened from the road by trees, where they kept their horses. From there they would secretly take their horses to be shod by a smith at Fifield – leaving them overnight and collecting them in the morning, throwing a few coins at the smith. They would plot their nefarious deeds at the Bird in Hand at Cap's Lodge – a den of iniquity if ever there was one. Not far from it is Habbergallows Hill, where stood the gibbet oak – the lonely tree where several of their acquaintances swung in the wind. You would think this alone would have kept them on the straight and narrow, but alas it didn't.

The Dunsdons' career in crime started small-time, following farmers home from market and relieving them of their purses, the contents of which they'd often end up drinking at the Bird in Hand. But drunk on success, they grew bolder. They needed to do something that would make them stand out from the lower class of criminal; something that would secure their reputation as the 'Kings of the Outlaws of Wychwood'. Then they got wind of the Oxford to Gloucester coach, which was carrying a coffer containing the princely sum of five hundred pounds. They lay in wait for the coach and, disguised with black scarves around their features, they boldly held it up; all swagger and bluster. Everything went to plan and they escaped with their booty. Hiding their horses in the secret cave at Icomb, they were never caught.

But it is often said that pride comes before a fall.

How could they top that?

Well, it seemed fickle fortune smiled.

They had heard of the riches of Tangley Manor – a carrot too fat to ignore – and one night, over a tankard or three, they planned their robbery. Unfortunately, this was overheard and the butler was tipped off. The butler in turn called the constables to the manor on the night of the planned robbery and they lay in wait behind the main door as Tom, Dick and Harry approached – thinking the Lord was away, leaving only his wife and children.

Slyly, Dick reached in through a slot used to spy on visitors. He had been told that the key hung on a string within reach of this. He groped about in the dark, sticking in his arm as far as it would reach. The constables were waiting and one of them quickly tied a rope around the trespassing limb – pulling it tight. Dick cried out, warning his brothers. The constable's rattles went a-clacking, raising the alarm. Others came running along the passages of the house, and from around the outside – their boots crunching on the gravel. Dick tugged and tugged, but couldn't pull his arm free. He knew there was only one thing for it. 'Cut it off! Cut it off!' His brothers hesitated, but there was no time to waste. One of them did the deed, accompanied by a sibling scream of agony, and the arm dropped down inside the front door, the rope still attached to it. For a moment it twitched, then lay still. The brothers escaped – Dick wailing and trailing blood. Tom and Harry managed to escape, but Dick was never seen again, so perhaps he bled to death before they could reach their horses and ride back to their secret cave.

Tom and Harry laid low for a while, in fear of their lives, or mourning their brother – or perhaps both. But the lure of breaking the law could not be resisted for long, and in 1784 they were finally caught when their bragging got the better of them.

They were at the Bird in Hand at the time of the Capp's Lodge Fair day – they must have been doing some serious drinking for they started bragging loudly that they were the Highwaymen of Wychwood Forest and no one would ever catch them. The landlord, in jest, said he could take the pair of them himself. They goaded him, so he had a go – one of them fired a pistol but his apron-full of change saved the landlord's life. The other men in the gambling house took umbrage at this – shooting the landlord was not on! They seized the drunken brothers and they were frogmarched to Gloucester, where they were tried and hung – their bodies brought back in an old farm cart to swing on the gibbet oak at Habbergallows, a warning to all.

And so Tom, Dick and Harry met their grisly end: the Highwaymen of Wychwood Forest, swinging high.

Perhaps the brothers – and wayward limbs – were finally reunited, riding their old haunts together: mad, bad and damned until the end of time; a lesson to the curious, that crime can pay, but it exacts a very high price.

This bloodthirsty tale is made even more thrilling for being true. Whether the saying about 'any old Tom, Dick or Harry' originated from it, who knows? Of course, there are more famous highwaymen, chief amongst them Dick Turpin, whose story was transformed by popular culture; but the reality was far less glamorous and travellers would cross the Wychwood Forest at their peril. These days, there are fewer past-times more pleasant than a day out in the Cotswolds, exploring the back lanes and stopping at charming country pubs – such as the Bird in Hand pub at White Oak Green: the location of the original Habbergallows perhaps?

Seventeen

MOLLIE AND THE CAPTAIN

The elegant town of Henley-on-Thames, home of the famous Regatta – the epitome of respectable Middle England – is the last place you would expect to find a crime of passion occurring. It is simply not the place where people rock the boat – let alone murder their loved ones, but that is what happened in the summer of 1751.

Blandy, the Town Clerk of Henley, had a daughter, Mary (or Mollie, as she was known) who made up in dowry what she lacked in physical charm. Mollie was now twenty-six and still unmarried – for the times, practically over the hill – because her father had been 'choosy' for her, only wanting the best (or the richest). Until her father found her a 'suitable suitor' Mollie would remain un-worshipped.

Finally, when they had all but given up, they thought they had found a match, thanks to the help of a General Kerr.

Kerr introduced them to 'Captain, the Honourable' William Cranstoun, descended from a Scottish peer: forty-six, unhand-some, pock-marked, small – yet he had a certain charm of manner and a title. So, despite being impoverished this didn't put Blandy off and was pleased when Cranstoun showed interest in Mollie.

The Captain, stationed in Henley, became a frequent visitor to the Blandys as he set to wooing Mollie. She was not unwilling. Mrs Blandy was happy with the courtship – of ill health, she wanted her daughter wed to an eligible suitor and bearing her grandchil-dren before she shuffled off this mortal coil.

However, there was a catch.

Kerr discovered Cranstoun was already married to a certain Anne Murray in Edinburgh! Because she was a Catholic and the daughter of a Jacobite family, Cranstoun had kept the marriage a secret to avoid it affecting his chances of promotion. When he had been ordered south, his wife returned to her family home, with their daughter.

You can imagine the heated conversations in the Blandy house-hold when this revelation was discovered. It looked like Mollie's hopes of love were doomed – for she did love him, despite eve-rything. After all, he had given her a brooch made of Scottish pebbles, declaring his love for her.

Cranstown somehow managed to persuade the Blandys that he wanted the marriage annulled and was optimistic that this would happen soon.

Then tragedy struck. Mrs Blandy died. Mr Blandy was beside himself with grief.

Cranstoun was recalled for duty to Scotland but Mollie still did not give up on her suitor. Mr Blandy felt differently. Was the Captain a fortune hunter? He forbade Mollie to have anything more to do with Cranstoun but, alas, he was too deep in her heart.

Cranstoun sent Mollie a gift of some white powder, apparently to 'clean the pebbles'. It was, in fact, a 'love potion', as he put it, which would 'soften her father's heart'. All she needed to do was add it in secret quantities to his food. Mollie agreed – so blindly was she in love. Mr Blandy's health deteriorated rapidly, for Mollie was unwittingly poisoning her father with arsenic! When they realised the truth she was as distraught as he. In floods of tears, Mollie confessed all to her dying father and with his last breath he forgave her.

The court and the folk of Henley were less forgiving about the murder of their Town Clerk.

When the doctor came to examine Blandy and announced the verdict of death by suspicious circumstances, Mollie gave him the slip. The doctor raised a hue and cry and soon a mob was hounding for Mollie's blood as she raced along the streets of respectable Henley.

Heart pounding, Mollie raced towards the river bridge, under which stoically flowed Old Father Thames – whose banks had bore witness to many tragedies. For a moment she considered throwing herself into his cold embrace. What had life brought her but misery? Both her parents were dead and her lover – what nature of man or devil was he?

Seeing the pathetic figure of Mollie weeping by the riverbank, the landlady of The Angel public house took pity on her and gave her shelter from the mob. Lord knows what might have happened if they had lain their hands on her in the midst of their frenzy. But when the Justices of the Peace arrived, she was finally apprehended and brought to justice.

Mary Blandy was put on trail for the murder of her father on 29th of February 1752. She pleaded innocence – claiming she did not know the true nature of the powder given to her by the Captain. She listened stony-faced to her accusers and to her sentence – to be hanged by the neck until she was dead. Some took her lack of expression as evidence of her guilt, but there were many there who thought otherwise. It was clear to all who knew her how much she had loved her father. And who has not been made a fool of by love?

Awaiting her execution she was given privileges and her friends came to visit her. Many remarked at the stoic grace with which she calmly accepted her fate. Then, on 6th of April 1752, she was hanged until she was dead. The young virginal body of the late Ms Blandy was buried at midnight in the local church, between her parents. Despite the late hour, many came to witness the sad end of Mary. A lot of people believed her innocent of poisoning her father – a victim of the so-called 'Captain, the Honourable'.

As for the cad Cranstoun – he fled to the Continent, to the Flemish town of Furnes, where he died in agony in December … apparently poisoned by arsenic. By whom, remains a mystery. Was it Kerr? A citizen of Henley? Another spurned lover? Perhaps justice was delivered after all – in a dish served up cold.

This heartbreaking tale is a true story. The trial and execution of Mary Blandy was recorded at the time, and a moving contemporary account of the execution appeared as Appendix VII of William Roughead's Trial of Mary Blandy (1914). The location of her execution was either the Westgate prison mound or in the Castle Yard in Oxford – both of which are very close to each other. According to folklore, a blackbird was perched on the gallows during her execution and from that date no blackbird has been heard to sing in that vicinity. It is hard to imagine such a scandalous crime happening in the pleasant river-town of Henley-on-Thames, but it just goes to show that you can never judge by appearances!

Eighteen

FAIR ROSAMUND'S BOWER

From the moment he laid eyes upon her he had to have her. It was as simple as that. Henry II was known for his liking of the ladies – his wife, Eleanor of Aquitaine, certainly knew – but he had never beheld such a beauty before as the aptly named Rosamund: the rose of the world.

The daughter of the marcher lord, Walter de Clifford, and his wife Margaret Isobel de Tosny, Rosamund grew up in the wooded folds of the Wye Valley, in Clifford Castle. Seemingly protected from the world by the winding gorge, it was a fairytale place to spend a childhood – but childhood must come to an end. And one day, when Rosamund was in the bloom of her young womanhood, it did, when the King passed by her father's castle during one of his campaigns against the troublesome Welsh. There always seemed to be a rebellion to quell in those days.

It was Christmas and it was Clifford's duty to entertain the King. And Henry was in the mood for merry-making. His wife had given birth to John, who was to be their last child, on Christmas day. Their marriage had soured after many children and many affairs. It was a familiar pattern. The screaming, smelly baby; the moody, mardy wife; the claustrophobia of court – he had to get away. Even dealing with surly rebels in the damp Welsh valleys was more appealing than being stuck at home.

Rosamund had the most beautiful hair he had ever beheld – long and soft and fair. Her skin was as pale as milk; her eyes as bright as morning. She was the stuff of troubadour songs. While Henry was entertained in Clifford's hall, he couldn't take his eyes from her, she was so graceful. Clifford noticed Henry's attentions and knew his reputation, but he did not raise a finger to prevent what was happening, instead adding kindling to a fire. It was inevitable; perhaps he thought it would be advantageous. His daughter, the sweetheart of the King – just imagine – it would win him favour and gain him influence. Little did he know what unhappiness it would bring to them all.

Henry wooed Rosamund and she did not resist. The monarch could be wildly romantic. He had fashioned the grounds of Woodstock after the tale of Tristan and Isolde. There he had a picturesque bower made for Rosamund – a fairytale palace, hidden within a labyrinth. To this romantic fastness, away from the eyes of the world, he would come in secret, showering her with gifts and the sweet nothings of the heart. He talked of how there was no love in his marriage anymore, how Eleanor was ambitious and cold.

Her only appetite was for information, land and allies. She was respected and feared across Europe – the most powerful woman of the age. She was eleven years older than Henry and they had been together for fifteen years. She has borne him children, as a dutiful wife – heirs to the throne no less – but her husband's way-ward nature had proven too much, and she moved back to Poitiers, taking half the court with her. The Royal marriage bed was empty. No wonder Henry's eye was roving – so he reasoned to Rosamund.

But other eyes were also watching. Eleanor's spies. They noticed the King going back and forth into the bower, hidden in the 'wil-derness' of Woodstock, which he had filled with leopards and lions to enhance the effect. They reported this to Eleanor, who had been staying at Beaumont Palace, near Oxford, where she had given birth to John. The Queen went there herself to investigate, leaving her babe with the Royal wet nurse.

It was not the milk of human kindness that flowed in Eleanor's breast as she approached her husband's love-nest at Woodstock. Fierce creatures roamed the grounds, but none were as deadly as she; a woman scorned. With a small retinue of soldiers, Eleanor ventured deep into the forest, which was planted like a labyrinth – its many twists and turns designed to disorientate any casual visitor – but she was determined, and not without her wits. Her intel-ligence was renowned and an intelligent woman was dangerous!

She spotted a silken thread snagged on a branch. She recognised it as the kind that belonged to a certain needlework chest – once offered to her, now to his mistress. Furious, she followed this clue and came to the bower. There she came upon the young woman, sewing in the sunlight, guarded by a solitary knight – who was quickly overpowered by her men.

She confronted her rival. *This* was what had lured Henry from their marriage bed? A young slip of a maid, though she doubted she was a maid any more. She was pretty, in her way, but witless, going by her blathering protests of innocence – and docile; easier for Henry to manage. She laughed contemptuously.

Implacable, she offered Rosamund a choice between a dagger and a cup of poisoned wine. Rosamund looked at the Queen in horror. Was this to be her fate? What had she done wrong? She had only followed her heart; she had only wanted to make Henry happy. But in her heart of hearts she knew that what she had done was reprehensible. She had wanted the status of being Henry's lover – secretly craving what Eleanor possessed: her husband; a title; children; power; wealth; and influence. Be careful what you wish for, they say, as here was Eleanor before her – furious, and rightly so. She was only getting what she deserved.

Rosamund sighed, and bowed her head. Begging Eleanor's for-giveness, she accepted her fate. 'Let me take a drink from your cup.'

'You shall find it bitter,' replied Eleanor.

Rosamund had only known sweetness in her life. Perhaps it was time she tasted bitterness.

Fair Rosamund chose the poison and died in the bower that Henry had made for her, and that was the end of her.

Or so the story goes.

* * *

Eleanor was forever cast as the 'hard woman'; Rosamund the hap-less heroine – the victim of a dangerous game.

Yet that wasn't quite how it was. When news of the affair became public in 1174, Rosamund retired to Godstow Nunnery. The attention she was getting was becoming unbearable. Gerald of Wales wrote a scathing public attack on her character. His real target was Henry – because of the King's frequent wars against Wales – but the main casualty was Rosamund. He mocked the King's mistress as Rosa-immundi, 'Rose of Unchastity'. For Rosamund it was too much, and she brought the affair to a close. She joined her sisters at Godstow Nunnery and did not hear from the King again. It was as though she had vanished from the world. Inside the cloistered walls, she was unaware of the rumours swirling around the country of her apparent murder – a neat fiction to explain the end of the affair, perhaps even crafted by Henry himself and spread by his men, to slander his heartless wife, who had, in truth, murdered love.

Behind the veil at Godstow, Rosamund lived out the remainder of her days in virtuous chastity, reflecting upon her 'sins'. She found a peace there, a lasting happiness, at one with the Lord. As fair as she was in secular life, refined she became in the spiritual – her soul sifted by a simple, disciplined cycle of prayer, work and contemplation. When she died, she was buried with great honour. Henry, who had never forgotten her, and the Clifford family, paid for her tomb in the choir of the convent's church, and for an endowment that would ensure care of the tomb by the nuns. Her grave would become a shrine for many young women who took solace in her fall and return to grace; until her bones were removed by an over-zealous St Hugh, Bishop of Lincoln.

While visiting Godstow, Hugh of Lincoln noticed Rosamund's tomb right in front of the high altar. The tomb was laden with flowers and candles. The bishop was outraged at the worship of 'Rosamund the harlot', and ordered her remains removed from the church.

She was to be buried outside the church 'with the rest, that the Christian religion may not grow into contempt, and that other women, warned by her example, may abstain from illicit and adulterous intercourse.'

The nuns moved her relics in a perfumed leather bag to the cemetery by the Chapter House. Here, Henry, her father and many others would come to remember her until the nunnery was destroyed in the Dissolution of the Monasteries under Henry VIII.

Towards the end of the sixteenth century, a German traveller recorded the inscription, faded but still visible on the tombstone:

Let them adore ... and we pray that rest be given to you, Rosamund.

This is followed by a cruel rhyming epitaph: 'Here in the tomb lies the rose of the world, not a pure rose; she who used to smell sweet, still smells – but not sweet.'

Yet when her tomb was opened, there was said to be the scent of crushed roses. Rosamund – fair in life, fair in death.

Blenheim Palace is a locus of extraordinary historical significance. Centuries apart, it is where Winston Churchill was
born in 1874: he followed in the footsteps of his ancestor, John
Churchill, 1st Duke of Marlborough, who was given Blenheim
and its two thousand acres (the manor of Woodstock) by Queen
Anne and a 'grateful nation' following his famous victory at the
Battle of Blenheim in 1704. The lake was used in preparations
for the D-Day landings. Henry had landscaped the garden to
tell the story of the doomed lovers, Tristan and Isolde (later to
be enhanced by Capability Brown). Many romances have been
inspired by this tragic tale and the stories and speculation about
Henry's mistress continues to this day.

Nineteen

DOWN BY A
CRYSTAL RIVER SIDE

Near Woodstock town in Oxfordshire
As I walked for to take the air
To view the fields and meadows round
Me thought I heard mournful sound.

Down by a crystal river side,
A gallant bower I espied,
Where a fair lady made great moan,
With many a bitter sigh and groan.
(From 'The Oxfordshire Tragedy', or 'Near Woodstock Town')

Once, there was a handsome young nobleman from Oxfordshire called Robert, who married a comely young maid called Amy. They were both young, beautiful and brimming with life, and it felt like the world was their oyster. Deep in love, all things were possible and the future was theirs. Alas, tragedy was to strike and their fate was to be no fairytale.

Robert Dudley was the fifth son of John Dudley, Duke of Northumberland, and Jane Guildford, and he was always destined for great things. There was something in his manner, the way he held himself and later, as a handsome young man, the dashing figure he cut. Women admired him and men wanted to be like him. He was to catch the eye of the most powerful woman in the land; but at the age of eighteen he was besotted with Amy Robsart. She was the woman who had won his heart. He wooed her and married her, for who could refuse him? For a while they lived in happiness. It was like a dream come true.

But Robert was often called away to court – more often than Amy would like. However happy they seemed to be when they were together, she could not help fretting about all the fine pretty ladies at court – who no doubt flirted with him. He placated her with soft words, reassuring her that her heart was safe with him. She was the only woman in the world that mattered – the love of his life! Amy would watch him gallop away, clutching her breast.

These were dramatic, dangerous times. There were many intrigues at court, which Robert became involved in. He was never able to discuss these with Amy, for her own safety, and so his comings and goings were often veiled in secrecy. Only later did it come to light how deep he was involved in not only courtly intrigues, but the deadliest of games. Robert supported his father in the vain attempt to place Jane Grey on the throne in July 1553, and was condemned to death for doing so; dark times indeed.

It was only when he was facing execution that Robert was able to reveal his part in the plot to his wife, who had, through her influence and wealth, been able to arrange a brief, private visit to him in the Tower. She thought that would be the last she would ever see of him and she left as though she herself was walking to the block.

Robert's father lost his head for his part in the plot – a deadly blow to them all – but then a miracle occurred and Robert was pardoned. That was October 1554. For his own good, he went abroad and distinguished himself with his brother in the campaign against France in 1557. He received some kindness from Queen Mary's husband, Philip II of Spain, but his real fortunes began when Elizabeth, upon her accession, made him her Master of the Horse.

And so Robert returned to England in glory. He was the Faerie Queen's chosen one. Some wicked gossips said he was her suitor. Amy tried to ignore such cruel words – for did he still not come back to her, a loyal husband? And the Queen and her Master of the Horse was often heard arguing most passionately. Some speculated that Queen Bess bore little love for him, but used him as a stalking horse – to deter other suitors who were eager to win her hand and her vast wealth, power and lands. At the end of the day, these were all words, idle speculation – for what did it matter, as long as her beloved Robert was back in her bed, well, most nights?

But then in 1560, on a dark night, tragedy struck. The exact nature of events is still a mystery, but the facts are plain enough. On the 8th of September of that year, at Cumnor Place, in Oxfordshire, Amy was found dead, lying at the foot of the stairs with a broken neck. Some say that she died of a broken heart; others say that she was murdered by her husband, the Queen's favourite, Robert Dudley, Earl of Leicester. Of course, Robert played the grieving widower very convincingly and performed all the necessary rites.

And yet, the death of his wife was all too convenient, for it cleared the way for him to marry Queen Elizabeth – the greatest of prizes. Although this powerful union failed to manifest, there was still plenty of evidence to suggest Robert was the Queen's chosen one: she rewarded him with rich gifts of Crown lands and, in a moment of weakness, she named him Protector of the Realm in the event of her death, when she had her only recorded illness in 1562.

Whatever the circumstances and motives of Amy's death, Robert, having observed the etiquette of grieving, set forth to marry the Queen by all means available to him. He told Spanish ambassadors that he would bring England back to Catholicism if Philip would help him to her hand. And so, he was considerably flabbergasted when the Queen gravely proposed him as a husband for her rival, Mary Queen of Scots. In order to fit him for the post, she created him, in 1564, Earl of Leicester.

He should have been pleased.

His career should have taken off after that, but it was far from glorious – his relations with the Queen were strained and perhaps the result of a painful game they played with each other, behaving and appearing to the entire world like spurned lovers.

The wounded heart is the most savage of beasts.

Dudley owned Cornbury Park, near Woodstock town. When life at court got too much, he often enjoyed hunting there. Things had got rather difficult of late and although he had done his best to defend the realm against the Spanish, his attempts had not always been successful or appreciated. He had been accused of extravagance and incompetence in his command of the Queen's Troops, and yet had she not entrusted him with them at Tilbury in August 1588, when the defeat of the Spanish Armada was yet hardly known? Perhaps that elusive Faerie Queen still held a candle for him in secret? Did true love ever truly die? He was pondering this one day in late summer, as he was riding through the golden forest of Cornbury, the sunlight shimmering through the canopy, when a pale figure suddenly appeared before him, making his horse shy and throwing him from his saddle. Momentarily stunned, he brushed the mulch from his face and gasped – before him was his former wife!

'Amy … is that you?'

It was the very image of his late wife and yet there was something about her that was unnatural. The way she stared so; the angle of her neck; the pallor of her skin. She pointed at Robert – rooting him to the spot. 'Husband, my grave is cold. You will join me, ten days' hence, to warm it in your winding shroud.' And then she vanished. Robert tried to laugh it off. Surely it was just a pool of sunlight through the trees? The Master of the Horse remounted and rode off. Thinking to himself nothing broken; no harm done.

And yet, ten days later, Amy's prophecy came true. On the 4th of September 1588, exactly ten days after seeing the ghost – for surely that is what it was – Robert Dudley, Earl of Leicester, died; the cause of death a mystery.

Amy's ghost is said to have appeared at Cornbury several times since these tragic incidents, warning again of sudden death. The house was pulled down in 1810, 'because her ghost gave the locals so much trouble.' The tragic tale of Robert and Amy appears to have been recorded in a popular ballad, originating around 1736-63, entitled *The Oxfordshire Tragedy*, or *Near Woodstock Town*:

Alas! quoth she, my love's unkind,
My sighs and tears he will not mind,
But he is cruel unto me,
Which causes all my misery.

Soon after he had gained my heart
He cruelly did from me part;
Another maid he does pursue,
And to his vows he bids adieu.

The green turf served her as a bed,
And flowers a pillow for her head;
She laid her down and nothing spoke,
Alas! For love her heart was broke.

Soon after was the squire possessed
With various thoughts that broke his rest,
Sometimes he thought her groans he heard,
Sometimes her ghastly ghost appeared.

'Since my unkindness did destroy
My dearest love and only joy
My wretched life must ended be;
Now must I die and come to thee!'

His rapier from his side he drew
And pierced his body through and through,
So he dropped down in purple gore
Just where she did some time before.

He buried was within the grave
Of his true love – and thus you have
A sad account of his hard fate,
Who died in Oxfordshire of late.

Twenty

THE OXFORD STUDENT

There was once an Oxford student who wooed the daughter of a local brewer of the town. Famed for her looks, she was regarded as the comeliest wench to serve a flagon of ale and brought customers flocking to her father's hostelry. She was not dismissive of the scholar's attentions and they began courting, one thing led to another, and the inevitable happened – the student got her with child.

She pressed him to marry her, to make an honest woman of her – something he, with sly tongue, always put off while convincing her of his sincere intentions and undying love. But, at last, he said that if she would meet him at Divinity Walk the next moonlight night, he would arrange it.

So, early on the night of the next full moon, the brewer's daughter set out for the open orchard land that bordered Divinity Walk in those days. She was very early, so for safety – for they were rough times – she climbed one of the apple trees and hid there. Presently she heard heavy steps, and saw her lover plodding up the hill with a spade across his shoulders. He came up to the very tree where she was hiding and began to dig a long, narrow, deep hole. Then he stood and waited with a dagger in his hand and a dark look upon his face. But the girl, lying along the branch above him, never stirred, and at length he went away, and she ran as fast as her feet could carry her back to her father's house. Next day, as she was going down Brewer's Lane, the student saw her, and greeted her lovingly. Up piped the brewer's daughter, who sang:

One moonshiny night, as I sat high,
Waiting for one to come by,
The boughs did bend; my heart did break,
To see what hole the fox did make.

As she sang her strange song, the student whipped out his dagger and, stunning her into silence, stabbed her deep in the heart.

The villain fled, leaving the broken body of his victim, her heart weeping blood.

It was well known about the affection the brewer's daughter had for this scholar, for she did nothing but talk of it to her friends, and it was not long for the prime suspect to be identified.

When news of this scandalous murder got out there was the greatest fight between town and gown that ever was known:

Brewer's Lane ran with blood. The cruel student was killed in the melee; the mob were sated, their brutal justice administered – but nothing would bring the poor girl back to life.

They say she was buried in the very grave that was dug for her by her false lover – the final resting place of the brewer's daughter.

This tale was derived from Halliwell's Nursery Rhymes and Tales. *The nefarious student here is the type mocked in the ballad* The Oxford Scholar *(1813–29). One of the verses seems particularly apt:*

A servant maid I always kept
To sweep out my study and chamber,
I could kiss her when I liked
Because I could command her;
But sure such havoc I did make
Withal to dress my honour,
I was a most wild and extravagant rake,
When I was an Oxford scholar.

Twenty-one

WASHINGTON AND THE CHERRY TREE

George loved his hatchet – the way it felt in his hand, the carved wooden handle, the sharp cold edge which he would nervously run his finger along. Holding it, he felt like a Big Chief – although in fact, he was only six. He ran through the leafy grounds of Sulgrave Manor, his family home, hollering Apache-style and scaring the bejeezus out of squirrels. This was his tribal territory, and he was master of it – a fearsome scout. Nothing moved here without his knowledge. The comings and goings of his family; their visitors; the servants; the workers in the fields – he would watch them in secret from one of his hide-out trees. The people, the animals, the buildings and fields – why, it seemed to be a perfect corner of God's kingdom. Everybody and everything seemed to have its place, its role, and yet some things seemed … less equal than others. As a six-year-old boy he was painfully aware of this. Although he was his father's son, he was still low down the pecking order. People talked over his head as though he wasn't there! His hair was ruffled, his cheek was pinched fondly, an old lady would give him a sweet, a man would bounce him on his knee, but he felt like he was some kind of pet. Why couldn't he be treated the same as the older boys – the farmhands, the servants – given roles and tasks and taken seriously?

A redskin in his rage, he leapt down and ran until he came to his father's favourite cherry tree – a fine young specimen it was. What drew him to it, he could not say, but before he knew it he was striking into it with his small axe in vexation. He. Wanted. To. Be. Equal. The hatchet made a satisfying thud each time, and gouged out a V of bark. He followed this line around the trunk until he had made a pale ring. He looked at it with pride, breathing hard. He wiped the sweat from his brow with his sleeve. His anger had passed, but at what price? A sick feeling in his guts made him run back to his den. For a while he brooded there, but his stomach growled. He couldn't be an outlaw for long. He had to go and hand himself in.

George left his 'mountain fastness' and returned to the main house, expecting to be clapped in irons. Yet everyone went about their business as usual. In the kitchens, he filched a cookie, fresh from the oven, and ran off before the cook could scold him. He seemed to have got away with it!

Then, a couple of days later, his father returned from business and was informed of the fate of his favourite cherry tree; that some thoughtless vandal had barked it. In fury, he called the servants to the main hall, had them all line up, and paced back and forth, waiting for the guilty culprit to confess. They held their heads in what seemed to be shame. 'Who has done this deed? It must be someone within our walls, for no other is admitted onto our grounds.' None of the servants spoke up, but they quaked in their boots.

George couldn't stand it any longer. He had been standing to one side, with his family, watching the whole spectacle. His father had insisted they were present – an attack on the cherry tree was an attack on the Washingtons. Still no one spoke.

'No one leaves this room until the guilty person owns up. If you are hiding the suspect, or have knowledge of him, then speak now, or you too shall be for the chop.'

One of the maids stifled a giggle. The housekeeper scowled at her. Just then George, with his little hatchet in his hand, stepped forward, shaking a little, but he tried not to show it.

'Yes, son, what is it? Can't you see I'm busy?'

George plucked up his courage and finally blurted out his shameful confession, 'I cannot tell a lie, father. I did it!'

His father looked at him with astonishment, as did the whole room.

George held up 'exhibit A'. 'I cut it with my hatchet. I cannot say why exactly. It just happened. I am sorry, father.'

His father snorted in disbelief, looked around at the other adults, pointing at his son in amazement, and then his harsh expression melted into a smile.

'Son, come here.' He gathered his son up into his arms. 'My son, that you should not be afraid to tell the truth is worth more to me than a thousand trees!'

From that day on George learned the value of living a truthful way and seeing justice done. Little did he know the seeds were sown that day for his future destiny: to become the President of the United States of America.

However apocryphal this tale, it is so famous and so charming, that it simply had to be included. A visit to Sulgrave Manor itself will bring alive Washington's 'backstory' in a more factual way. What I find intriguing is the thought that some of his family's servants might have taken part in the local Mummers' Play

– *the text of which has survived – or that George himself might have witnessed it at Christmas-tide. On the 3rd of December 1992, the Sulgrave Mummers play was once again performed in the Great Hall of the Manor House, with parts played by members of the local history society. Since then, it has been revived in Northampton in an updated version by storyteller Jo Blake Cave and friends. The Mounts Mummers performed it on Christmas Eve 2011 around the town, culminating on the steps of All Saints' Church; a modern, motley crew of characters (Molly; Duke of Cumberland; King George; Dr Parr; Jack Finney; Baalzebub; Bighead) akin to those George himself might once have seen in the grounds of his British ancestral home.*

Twenty-two

A STITCH IN TIME – THE WEAVERS OF WITNEY

Progress is not always a good thing. Things get smaller, faster, flashier – but at twice the price, and lasting half as long. Sometimes newer isn't always bestter, and something of the texture of life can be lost. In the Cotswolds, the warp and weft of community is strong in the old wool towns. Witney is one such place – proud of its weaving heritage and its world-famous blankets. Queen Anne appointed a weaver by the name of John White as the master of the Company of Blanket Weavers, granted a charter in 1711. Thomas Early assumed his mantle when he passed on – the Earlys had long been associated with weaving in the town. In 1669, Richard Early apprenticed his fourteen-year-old son, Thomas, to the woollen trade. Three hundred years later, their blankets were still being made and sold on both sides of the Atlantic.

The tradition of weaving has endured in Witney – like the family ties stretching back generations – but times change. The weavers of the town were not happy with the new technology which threatened their livelihoods. Faced with the spectre of unemployment, lacking the security blanket of the Welfare State – they took to sabotaging the machines that started to make their appearance in the early nineteenth century. The lives of the employers were

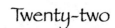

threatened and riots broke out both in the streets and the fields –
farmworkers equally besieged by the new machines. Yet the forces
of progress and commerce could not be stopped.

In 1837, the waters of the river Windrush, which had turned
the mills and scoured the wool for decades, was replaced with
steam power.

In 1851, the Great Exhibition allowed John Early to show his
skill to the world – a patterned blanket won him a Bronze Medal
and a certificate signed by Prince Albert no less.

Yet another exhibition was causing greater interest; John Coxeter,
a woollen merchant of Newbury, boasted that on his new-fangled
machine (actually forty years old by that point) he could take a
coat from a man's back, reduce it to wool and make it into a coat
again, all within twenty-four hours – turning a coat into a coat,
such is the wonder of progress! Sir John Throckmorton of Buckland

approached Coxeter and asked if he could take the wool growing on a sheep's back at sunrise and make it into a coat by sunset the same day. He was willing to wager a thousand guineas on the project. Coxeter agreed to the challenge. On the morning of 25th of June 1811, Frances Druett, Sir John's shepherd, sheared two Southdown sheep as the sun rose, at 5 a.m. Eleven hours later, the dyed cloth was ready to be cut by James White, the son of a Newbury tailor. Nine men were waiting with needles threaded and by twenty minutes past six the coat was finished, with one hour and forty minutes left before sunset. That evening, Sir John dined with forty of his friends at the Pelican Inn at Speenhamland, wearing his fine new coat.

The Earlys of Witney challenged this record in 1906, when, on the 8th of June, sheep were shorn at sunrise, and ten hours and twenty-seven minutes later the blankets were completed, embroidered with a ducal 'M' and presented to the Duke of Marlborough. John Coxeter's record was finally broken, after nearly a century.

With the advance in technology further wonders were possible.

On the tercentenary of Thomas Early's apprenticeship (three hundred years earlier), on 11th of June 1969, they set about breaking their own record in Transatlantic style. At 4 a.m., one hundred and fifty Kerry Hill sheep were sheared. The wool passed through the necessary processes in record time, and the first blanket was ready at 12.11 p.m., eight hours and eleven minutes after shearing.

Before evening, fifty blankets were completed, one of which was flown to New York in time to be displayed with the notice: 'The wool of which this blanket is made was shorn from sheep at Witney, England, this morning.'

It was not the first time that Witney blankets had crossed to the New World – Native Americans were fond of them, notably the Indians of Virginia and New England, who liked the red and blue dyes. They would tear off suitable lengths, make two holes for their arms, and wrap the remainder around their bodies. In exchange, they brought furs to the English traders. Whether these Witney blankets contained the smallpox that decimated their population is not known.

* * *

Time flows on. The weaving industry floundered through the twentieth century and by the end was threadbare. Some filaments remain, but it is a shadow of its former glory. Now it is cheaper to import fabrics made in the sweatshops of China; ship them halfway across the world, like that transatlantic record-breaking attempt – but at what cost to the Earth? Perhaps these cheap fabrics carry with them their own kind of 'smallpox', decimating local industry and destroying communities. Yet some are realising the value of the local, the handmade, the ethically-sourced and lovingly crafted – as opposed to the mass-produced and shoddy.

Visit a Farmers' Market in the area these days, and you'll see stalls selling all kinds of fine wares. The looms and wheels are still at work in the homes of traditional artists. Perhaps the Fates have spared this particular thread.

Here's to the homespun; and to weaving the threads of life. Long may wool be gathered on the Cotswolds!

Wool was once the linchpin of the Cotswold economy; many of the towns developed as a result of its value, and Witney's story is not unique, however much the accomplishments of its inhabitants might be. Although the people of Witney have been trading in wool as far back as the Iron Age, it was the medieval period that really saw the wool trade boom. They truly believed that the secret to their success was that they had sheep that were a cross between the Iron Age sheep and a breed that the Romans brought to Britain resulting in long, fine wool, the quality of which made exporting easy. The land along the nearby Windrush River was used for bringing up sheep and the water helped in the many processes in cloth making. Witney also had good road networks to trading centres. Now we live in far more connected times, and

the procurement of goods from overseas is not seen as anything special, indeed, it has become the norm – often to the detriment of the local economy. Yet it seems, once more, that people are valuing the local and hand-made in the many splendid markets and craft shops across the region.

Twenty-three

MOWING
YARNTON MEADOWS

I remember the Mowing Fair from the meadows of summer as though it was yesterday. Old Gran Joan you may know me as, and a grandmother I'll always be to your strong eyes, but when the sun is on the grass I still feel like a little girl inside. Listen close, and I'll tell you my tale...

Once-a-time, the lush meadow of Yarnton was the scene of great festivity in July of each year. The whole village throbbed with excitement. It was the time for the drawing of lots for the common land, and the Mead Balls were used for this venerable custom. I might look old to you young pups, but these Mead Balls were the oldest relics in the village even then. Once, many a meadow had them, but now they seem to be the only surviving ones in England these days. Small, hard and tough – like me! – they have managed to survive. They were used when the Domesday Book was writ. Thirteen balls, made of a light wood – probably holly, one inch in diameter, worn smooth with constant handling – you could hold them in the palm of your hand. Look close and you'll see names scrivened on them – Boat, White, Dunn, William, Water Molly, Green, Boulton, Rothe, Gilbert, Harry, Freeman, Walter Jeoffrey and Parry – tenant farmers with mowing rights in the meadows. How far back they go, no one knows.

On the first Monday in July local farmers in the district, who, through being born and bred in the neighbourhood, have mowing rights in the meadows, assemble to draw the lots. They used to do this down on the meadow, but these days it transpires at the Grapes Inn – maybe too many wettings or not enough! The Head Meadsman arranges for the drawing of the Balls and for the cutting of the hay. He needs to be a sharp 'un for its a mighty fierce doings, measuring out the various lots. I'll try my best to describe it to you, so listen close.

The meadows were divided into strips known as customary acres – or as much as a man may mow in a day. Locally, this was called 'one man's mowth'. These strips were divided between the thirteen farmers whose names appeared on the original Balls. Then as the farms disappeared, and only eight remained in the village, the strips were absorbed by them. Consequently, some farmers had more hay than they required and so sold the surplus before the actual mowing day arrived and, when the Balls were drawn, the purchasers claimed the strips they had bought.

Following it so far?

Solemn as pallbearers, the two head meadsmen would then proceed to a certain spot in the meadow about to be mown – they would walk a stately pace, but that might have been just the cider. A Ball would be drawn from the bag, and its name loudly proclaimed. A man with a scythe would cut about six foot of hay in a few sweeps, and another man quickly cut out the initials of the claimant in the ground. Then they would all proceed to the next lot and a Ball would be drawn again and another man's initials inscribed amid the freshly mown hay. This continued until all the lots were marked and, all the while, another meadsman would carefully note down the details of each strip and its owner to avoid dispute later on. In order to distinguish the boundary between the strips, a number of men would tread up and down them – this was called running the treads.

The meadows had lovely names: Oxhay, Picksey (now Pixy), Little Hayday, Great Hayday, Big Couch, Little Couch, The Hope Yard, The Ship and West Mead. They lie on the north bank of Old

Father Thames – one hundred and seventeen acres I'm told. Eight of these were tithed to vicars and the scholars of Exeter College, and they were known as Tithals or Tidals.

There, you keep listening and you'll keep learning!

In order to cut the meadows in one day, which was no mean feat, about one hundred labourers were imported into the village. Large quantities of liquor were kept close by, and in the hedges – so that the thirsty men could stop frequently, quench their thirst, and carry on with renewed vigour. On the completion of the mowing, they were very merry indeed and the races, which always wound up the proceedings, were often run by many pairs of unsteady legs. The main race was for the honour of securing a garland, which the winner placed in the church, there to remain for one year.

Yet when men and drink mix, things soon turn foolish. The fair got rowdier and rowdier. Once, there were riots and a man was killed. That was a terrible day. The vicar preached fire and brimstone at us the following Sunday.

After that they spread the mowing over three days – to water it down, so to speak – and things became more civil.

I imagine a few of them rioters ended up at Stock Trees. Three mighty trees once grew there, by the village stocks. I remember them poor lads getting a proper pelting, and perhaps I joined in too. Garden refuse and rotten fruit, cowpats, the lot! Then they were marched across the road by old Farmer, the village constable with his black baton, to spend a night in the lock-up, a guest of the magistrate. That soon sobered 'em up!

Well, the wheel turns and village life gets back to normal pretty sharpish after the Fair days. Work to be done. The Mead Balls are put away 'til the following year.

We don't let the grass grow under our feet around here!

What? You cheeky so-and-so! Off with you, before I cuff you round the lobes. I'm not too old to cut you down to size. I'm a Yarnton girl. We know how to swing scythes round here.

Although the tradition at Yarnton has become a low-key affair, mowing fairs still take place in some parts of the country, such as the Somerset Scythe Fair – where one can get a flavour of times past. A mowing match is held there every summer. I have imagined the Mowing Fair at Yarnton from the point of view of one of the old villagers, based upon an account I read: Grandmothers' Tales, *a story by Joan Roe published around 1981 about Yarnton life. There is a curious footnote to all of this.*

Yarnton was known for many years as the grave of the mammoths. Records exist telling of enormous animals such as wild oxen, large deer and hippopotami, which roamed the district seeking water. It was at a time when the whole country was drying up, and eventually the only water left for them was in Portmeadow. There they assembled, a vast army of huge animals, awaiting their last drink. Such masses of bones and phosphate of lime has been found that geologists say the animals lay in heaps, and all died practically at the same time. And from the bones of dragons grows the good green grass of Yarnton meadow.

Twenty-four

THE OTMOOR UPRISING

I remember my father telling me all about it, as clear as yesterday. Did he take part in those September riots at St Giles Fair? So he did. Buy me a pint of Flowers and I'll tell you the long and the short of it...

It all started with a young upstart called Coke. Lord so-and-so stoked the fires alright. He wrote a scandalous pamphlet called ... let me get this right: 'A short view of the Possibility and Advantages of draining, dividing and enclosing Otmoor.' Wicked it was. Why? Because it would drive us off our land and take away our commoners' rights, to gather and graze fuel for hearth, fodder for cattle – that's why! Otmoor might not look much to the outsider; some call it a marshy wasteland! Can 'ee imagine? Well, perhaps you can, but on a summer day there's nowhere more lovely on God's good Earth. We'd drive our herds out there to pasture on the open plain; us littl' uns would tend the flocks of geese which loved to peck on the roughage; old nans scraped up the cow dung to sell for a few pennies; ducklings splashed in the pools; fish leapt in the streams, and, standing tall round it, the seven towns of Otmoor: Charlton, Oddington, Beckley, Noke, Horton, Fencott and Murcott. Like a kingdom unto itself. How could they take that away? Not without a fight, that's for sure...

And, by thunder, they got 'un!

We tore down Coke's notices wherever we saw 'em – made good kindling. Yet the young fool persisted. High and mighty, he would sound off so: 'To let four thousand acres of good land lie barren and desolate for about a dozen old women to pick up a scanty live-lihood from cow dung and goslings is too great an absurdity to be supported.' But supported it was – we got ourselves an ally in the form of Lord Abingdon no less, God bless him, who championed our corner. He stopped Coke's plan in court good and proper.

But the fool's plans would not go away – even when Coke did, to Nova Scotia. Had enough of us mardy Otmoors! When we get a feel-ing in our water, we're like the Moor-Evil – gets right into your bones on a claggy day. Nothing can shift 'un. And nothing can shift us!

It took 'em fourteen years to get started. The results of their folly was plain to see straight away – by playing with the drainage

they'd flooded the farmers' fields. My, they weren't happy, I can tell
'ee! They went in the dark and threw down them embankments!
Released the waters from the dykes. As soon as a fence was put up
it was thrown down again. There was that young hotspur Price,
whipping the men up with his fighting talk, here at The Crown
– used to be Higgs' Beerhouse back then. Josiah Jones, an outsider, came to stir up trouble even more. And even a gentleman,
Richard Smith, placed an appeal in the newspaper, which ruffled a
few feathers.

It wasn't long before there was a crowd of some say a thousand –
men, women, and children – walking out onto the moor together
in protest. What a sight it was! The whole moor was covered with
people tearing down fences; pulling up hedges; un-enclosing the
land. That was the summer of 1830. Everyone round here remem-
bers it. Harvest time. Back then, you could hear the scythes singing
through the fields – the whole village would put their backs into
it. And here we were, gathering in a different harvest. Yeomanry
arrived and arrested forty odd, carting them off to Oxford
Castle. But it just happened to be St Giles' Fair – first Monday in
September, the way it has been for centuries. There, the crowds
had been fired up by the likes of Price and Jones and were ready
for a fight. They chanted 'Otmoor forever!' again and again. Sticks
and stones started flying left, right and centre. The Guard struggled to frogmarch their prisoners through the press to the castle.
They were kicked and punched by men and women alike – my
father and me amongst them. It seemed like a great game to me.
A carnival. By the time they reached Beaumont Street the Yeoman
were in a sorry state and all their prisoners had slipped the collar.
Victory to the people!

How we sang and danced that night – drunk on success!

But we celebrated too soon. We had won the battle, but not
the war. They kept rebuilding the fences, planting the hedges, raising the banks, and, stubborn as mules, we kept pulling 'em down!
We got ourselves organised – under the cover of darkness and in
disguise small teams would go off 'on business'. I'd never forget
the times my father would come back with his face blacked up like

a mummer or, once, even dressed as a woman! They were handy, those night-raiders – once they tumbled a stone bridge!

The magistrates tried to recruit Parish constables to help patrol the moors, but no local would risk swearing in if he knew what was good for him. One of the constabulary was even on our side. A few backhanders here, a few pints there and it was 'business as usual'.

But that all changed when they brought in Layard of the Law – that's what they called him, though we called him something else – who whipped his team of fourteen into shape. It was hard to get away with the night-raids then. Nobody wanted to end up in gaol; or, worse, losing the roof over your head, what with mouths to feed and all. But there were concerns about the cost of this special constabulary defending what was, in effect, a private property speculation. The numbers were dropped to four and our raids began again in earnest – until the numbers were raised again. And so on. Right old game of cat and mouse it were!

This lasted for four years. But by 1835 the county no longer had a police force, for the rioting had ceased. The farmers had been talked round – they had their own property and land and liveli-hoods to worry about and couldn't risk losing it by being involved in anything illegal, like. Folk burn out, move on, or simply get old. Bones begin to ache until it's not so much fun, running around on a dark moor, in the mud and mist.

And so the protests died away. The moors were finally enclosed – Coke's fool-plan finally came true, twenty years on, but it never brought profit to the landowners, so, in a way, we were vindicated. The common folk had the common sense all along.

And to this day, the Otmoor uprising is remembered round these parts as an example of what folk can do when they work together and stand up to the foolish powers who are meant to rule us: 'Otmoor Forever!'

This historical story seems more pertinent than ever. I wrote it in the 'Year of Protest', 2011, when the Occupy movement was in full swing. To this the day in the area, the Otmoor Uprising is remembered with local pride in such places as The Crown Inn in Charlton-on-Otmoor – this was formerly Higgs' Beerhouse, the focal point of the rebellion. Here, on the 6th of September 1830, the locals organised their revolt, no doubt fuelled by the local brew and stirred up by the likes of Bartholomew Steer, a local carpenter who preached 'the politics of Cockayne', according to scornful accounts in the press. Then, as now, the press was used as a political weapon, but nothing could stem the tide of revolt. Never underestimate the power of the people!

Twenty-five

THE ROOFS OF BURFORD

The charmingly picturesque town of Burford – one of the gems of the Cotswolds – seems to be the quintessence of genteel middle England. Nothing seems to be out of place and one can imagine the status quo being maintained this way for decades; a pleasant, comfortable sleepiness. And yet the town has some dark stories in its history, revealing a different character to the town. Here are a couple.

* * *

Laurence Tanfield was born in the town in relatively poor circumstances, but through his own efforts and good fortune rose to the heights of society there. However, his story shows that success should not be gained at any cost and one should never forget one's roots.

His mother managed to get him educated for the Law; his own drive, industry and covetousness advanced him in wealth and dignity. He became sergeant-at-law; a judge; and, finally, Lord Chief Baron.

With his hard-earned wealth, Tanfield purchased and rebuilt Burford Priory, and in 1617 he bought the lordship of the manor and became first resident lord of the manor since the Norman

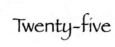

Conquest. How far he had come from his lowly birth! One would think such a reversal of fortune would make a man count his blessings and remember those who helped him on his way. Instead, the wealth and power seems to have turned Tanfield into a cruel-hearted tyrant.

The good citizens of Burford had come to regard their town as a Royal Borough – with its own privileges and rights – they were soon to learn how fickle Fortuna is. In 1620, a *quo warranto* was brought against the Burgesses of Burford by the Attorney-General and they were tried in a court presided over by Sir Laurence Tanfield. By its ruling, the Burgesses were stripped of their ancient rights.

Overnight, Tanfield made himself the most unpopular figure in town.

Hard-nosed as Tanfield was, harder still was his wife, Lady Tanfield. She was infamous for her dislike of the citizens of Burford, saying how she would like to grind them to powder beneath her chariot wheels. In a strange way, her wish came true.

The impact of the Lord Chief Baron's harsh ruling rippled out to the surrounding towns and villagers, so that the Tanfields were equally despised in Great Tew, Whittington and Wilcote. It was a great relief to the area when the Tanfields shuffled off this mortal coil. But if their wish was to rest in peace, it was not granted.

Lord Tanfield was sometimes seen haunting the backroads of Whittington in his spectral coach – the area became known as 'Wicked Lord's Lane'. It boded ill for whoever saw the coach.

And as for Lady Tanfield, she survived her husband by a few years – clinging onto life with the grim stubbornness with which she had coveted her wealth; but finally, she gave up the ghost. Yet even then, her spirit did not find rest. She was said to haunt the town, riding over the distinctive roofs of Burford in a fiery chariot, sometimes with Sir Laurence, foretelling any misfortune likely to overtake the town – like Hayley's Comet heralding the Norman Conquest.

In the eighteenth century, she became so troublesome that a band of seven clergymen came together to 'lay' her troublesome spirit to rest. They succeeded in calling her into church and conjuring her spirit into a bottle – which they corked securely before throwing it into the river, under the first arch. It was believed in times of drought, if the river level sank too low, and the arch ran dry, Lady Tanfield would rise again and once more ride over the roofs of Burford. One summer it was dry for so long, that the river began to 'hiss and bubble'. The citizens of Burford grew so concerned that they formed a human chain and poured pail after pail of water in from upriver, until, finally, the level started to rise, and the fiery spirit of Lady Burford was cooled once more, saving the town from the infuriating clattering of her chariot.

This tale bears a passing resemblance to that of 'Squire Crowdy of Highworth' – as related by Kirsty Hartsiotis in *Wiltshire Folk Tales* (The History Press, 2011). It seems Burford isn't the only village that has been forced to exorcise troublesome gentry!

ROUGH MUSIC

Another tale of Burford is far more down-to-earth, yet is another cautionary tale of marital hell…

Back in the day, legal divorce was costly and out of the range of poor folk – but there was another kind of separation involving the rough justice of the streets. It was commonly believed that a man, wishing to dispose of his wife for whatever reason, could put a halter around her neck and offer her for sale in the market place. This was sometimes a mutual arrangement agreeable to all parties, sealed with a drink in the local tavern and a couple of witnesses. But sometimes things weren't so amicable, and the husband would sell his wife to a stranger.

In 1855, a Burford man sold his wife at Chipping Norton market for the handsome sum of twenty-five pounds – half a crown was the usual going rate for a 'broken in' wife!

The cold-hearted husband lived in Simon Wisdom's Cottages at the bottom of town – down by the bridge. By this time, the town no longer considered this a civilised way to treat one's spouse and so, when word got out of this 'market-place divorce', for three nights running a crowd gathered down by his cottage and made 'rough music' with horns, trumpets, tin whistles and cans beaten with sticks. On the third night they burnt a straw effigy of the man outside his door. This was too much for the inhabitant and he burst out of his house with a pitchfork and thrust the mannequin into the river, and a good many of the crowd too.

Yet, when he had cooled down, the man reflected on his actions. Perhaps he had been too hasty, too harsh. He went back to Chipping Norton and there offered to buy his wife back for fifteen pounds, ten pounds less than he asked for originally: depreciation, of course!

This was recorded by Katherine Briggs, as related by a Mr Hambridge to his daughter, who, as a young boy, had been a part of the 'rough musicians' and had 'splashed through the river and escaped'. He never mentioned any names, for at the time he related the anecdote, 'some descendants of the people were still living'.

Burford saw even greater turmoil during the Civil War – three hundred and fifty Levellers were captured here as they rested on their way back from a disastrous skirmish with Lord Fairfax's troops at Salisbury. They were on their way to Banbury, but exhausted by their fight, were forced to rest.

Caught sleeping, they surrendered. Four of them were selected for execution. The ringleader capitulated and was pardoned at the eleventh hour. The others were not so lucky: the three Levellers were lined up in front of the church and shot on the 17th of May 1659; the round indentations of the bullet holes can still be seen – a chilling detail in an otherwise charming place.

Twenty-six

The Fisherman and His Wife

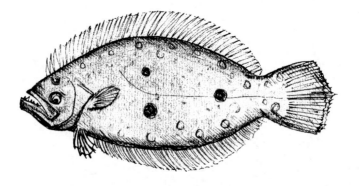

Not so long ago, a fisherman and his wife lived together in a ramshackle old place near Dorchester-on-Thames. Every day the fisherman went out with his rod and tackle and set up on his favourite spot on the river bank. It was more peaceful there. His wife was often complaining about this or that. Whatever he seemed to do, nothing was quite right for her. Gazing out over the waters, which so often seemed to reflect his mood, he hoped that his luck would change.

One time, he was sitting there fishing and looking out across the river, and he stared and stared – not thinking of anything, not feeling anything, just lost in the pattern of ripples and reflections, when, all of a sudden, his line gave a tug. And then another. Snapping out of his reverie, he gripped his rod and gave it a good pull. Up with a splash came his prize and he couldn't believe his eyes – he had caught a large, sparkly fish! He had never seen its like before, perhaps it had swum up the Thames from the sea. The truth was it was no ordinary fish. As it gasped for breath, the fish suddenly began to speak:

Fisherman, friend, I beg you – let me live! I am not an everyday kind of fish, as you can see, oh no! I'm a prince caught under an enchantment. It's true! Don't kill me! I won't taste good. Please, be so kind and put me back into the water, there's a good fellow. Let me swim free.

'Well, my! Who'd a thought it!' said the man. 'Maybe my luck has changed. One good turn deserves another. Don't say another word, Fish Prince! A fish who can talk deserves to live. There you go!'

With that he put his catch back into the clear water, and the fish quickly disappeared to the bottom, leaving a question mark of blood behind him.

Then the fisherman got up and went home to his wife in the hovel.

'Husband,' said the woman, 'didn't you catch anything today?'

'No. Yes…' replied the man.

His wife gave him one of her looks, fists on hips.

'I caught a fish, but he told me that … he was an enchanted prince … so I let him swim away.'

'What?' she fumed, rolling her eyes. 'Useless husband! Didn't you ask for anything first?'

'No,' he said quietly, a little ashamed. 'Umm, what should I have asked for?'

'Oh! What a husband!' she said, clapping her hand to her brow. 'Open your eyes. Look around you!'

The husband cast his eyes about, desperate to find some clue.

'Look at this place! It's a hovel. It stinks. It's filthy. You should have asked for a little cottage for us. Go back and call him! Go on!

Tell him what we want. A nice little cottage. He will surely give it to us.'

The man did not want to go, but neither did he want to oppose his wife, so, reluctantly, he went back to the river.

When he arrived there the water was no longer clear, but yellow and green. He stood there and said:

Little Man, Little Man, O hear me!
Big fish, little fish, swimming so free.
My wife, my strife, O hard-nosed Jill,
Wants not, wants not, what I will.

The water stirred as the sparkly fish popped up its head and said, 'What does she want then?'

'Oh, thank you!' breathed the man with a sigh of relief, 'I did catch you and kindly let you go, and now my wife says that I really should have asked for something. She doesn't want to live in a filthy shack any longer. She would like to have a cottage.'

The fish swished his tail. 'Go home, go home,' said the fish. 'She already has it.'

The man went home, and his wife was standing in the door of a cottage, and she said to him, 'Come in. See, now isn't this much better?'

There was a little front yard, a beautiful little parlour, a bedroom where their bed was standing, a kitchen, and a dining room. Everything was beautifully furnished and supplied with tin and brass utensils, just as it should be. And outside there was a little yard with chickens and ducks and a garden with vegetables and fruit.

'Ah, look at it all,' said the woman happily. 'Isn't this nice?'

'Yes,' said the man. 'This is quite enough. We can live here very well.'

'We will think about that,' said the woman.

Everything went well for a week or two, and then the woman said, 'Listen, husband. This cottage is too small. The yard and the garden are too little. The fish could have given us a larger house. I would like to live in … a large stone palace! Go back to the fish and tell him to give us a palace.'

'Oh, wife,' said the man, 'the cottage is good enough. Why would we want to live in a palace?'

'I know why. Men don't understand these things,' said the woman. 'Now you just go. The fish can do that.'

'Now, wife, the fish has just given us this cottage. I don't want to go back so soon. It may make him angry.'

'Just go,' said the woman. 'He can do it, and he won't mind doing it. Just go!'

The man's heart was heavy, and he did not want to go. He said to himself, 'This is not right,' but he went anyway.

When he arrived at the river the water was dark and surly. He stood on the shore and called out:

Little Man, Little Man, O hear me!
Big fish, little fish, swimming so free.
My wife, my strife, O hard-nosed Jill,
Wants not, wants not, what I will.

Up popped his sparkly friend. 'What does she want then?' asked the fish.

'Oh, I am embarrassed to say,' said the man. 'My wife isn't happy with the cottage. She now wants to live in … a stone palace.'

The fish swished his tail. 'Go home, go home. She's already standing before the door,' said the fish.

Then the man went his way, thinking he was going home, but when he arrived, standing there was a large stone palace. His wife was standing on the stairway, about to enter.

Taking him by the hand, she said, 'Come inside! Come and see!'

Inside the palace there was a large front hallway with a marble floor. Numerous servants opened up the large doors for them. The walls were all white and covered with beautiful tapestry. In the rooms there were chairs and tables of pure gold. Crystal chandeliers hung from the ceilings. The rooms and chambers all had carpets. Food and the very best wine overloaded the tables until they almost collapsed. Outside the house there was a large courtyard with the very best carriages and stalls for horses and cows.

Furthermore there was a magnificent garden with the most beautiful flowers and fine fruit trees and a pleasure forest a good half-mile long, with deer and hares and everything that anyone could possibly want.

'Now,' said the woman, 'isn't this nice?'

'Oh, yes,' said the man. 'This is quite enough! We can live in this beautiful palace and be satisfied.'

'We'll think about it,' said the woman. 'Let's sleep on it.' And with that they went to bed.

The next morning the woman woke up first. It was just daylight, and from her bed she could see the magnificent landscape before her. Her husband was just starting to stir when she poked him in the side with her elbow and said, 'Husband, get up and look out the window. Look, couldn't we be king over all this land?'

'Oh, wife,' said the man, 'why would we want to be king? I don't want to be king.'

'Well,' said the woman, 'even if you don't want to be king, *I* want to be king!'

'Oh, wife!' cried the man. 'Why do you want to be king? I don't want to tell him that.'

'Why not?' demanded the woman. 'Go there immediately. I must be king!'

So, reluctantly, the man went back, dragging his heels. 'This is not right, not right at all,' thought the man.

When he arrived at the river, it was dark grey – the water swelled restlessly and had a foul smell. He stood there and said:

Little Man, Little Man, O hear me!
Big fish, little fish, swimming so free.
My wife, my strife, O hard-nosed Jill,
Wants not, wants not, what I will.

Up popped the Fish Prince. 'What does she want then?'

'Oh, dear! Oh my!' wailed the man. 'Now she wants to be king!'

The fish swished his tail. 'Go home, go home. She is already king,' said the Fish Prince.

Then the man went home, and when he arrived there, the palace had become much larger, with a tall tower and magnificent decorations. Sentries stood outside the door, and there were so many soldiers, and drums, and trumpets. When he went inside everything was of pure marble and gold with velvet covers and large golden tassels. Then the doors to the great hall opened up and there was the entire court. His wife was sitting on a high throne of gold and diamonds, looking as pleased as punch. She was wearing a large golden crown and in her hand was a sceptre of pure gold and precious stones. On either side of her there stood a line of maids-in-waiting, each one a head shorter than the other.

'Oh, wife, are you now king?'

'Yes,' she said, 'now I am king!'

He stood and looked at her, shaking his head. Finally, he spoke: 'Wife, it is very nice that you are king. Now we don't have to wish for anything else.'

'No, husband,' she said, becoming restless. 'You are wrong! Time is on my hands. I cannot stand it any longer. Go to the fish. I am king, but now I must become … emperor!'

'Oh, wife!' cried the man. 'Why do you want to become emperor?'

'Husband,' she said, 'go to the fish. I want to be emperor!'

'Oh, wife,' said the man, 'he cannot make you emperor! We don't even have them in England! I cannot tell the fish to do that. Surely you are asking the impossible!'

'What!' said the woman. 'I am King, and you are my husband. Are you going? Go right this minute, I command you! If he can make me king then he can make me emperor. I am a modern woman and I can have everything. I want to be and simply have to be emperor – that's all there is to it. Go there immediately, or you'll lose your head!'

So he had to go. As he went on his way the frightened man thought to himself, 'This is not going to end well. To ask to be emperor is shameful. The Fish Prince is going to get tired of this.'

With that he arrived at the river. The water was black and dense and boiling. A strong wind blew over him that curdled the water. He stood there and said:

Little Man, Little Man, O hear me!
Big fish, little fish, swimming so free.
My wife, my strife, O hard-nosed Jill,
Wants not, wants not, what I will.

'What does she want then?' asked the fish.

'Oh, fish,' he said, a little embarrassed. 'My wife wants to become emperor.'

The fish swished his tail. 'Go home, go home,' said the fish. 'She is already emperor.'

Then the man went home, and when he arrived there, the entire palace was made of polished marble with alabaster statues and golden decoration. Soldiers were marching outside the gate, blowing trumpets and beating tympani and drums. Inside the house, barons and counts and dukes were walking around like servants. They opened the doors for him, which were made of pure gold. He went inside, where his wife was sitting on a throne made of one piece of gold a good two miles high, and she was wearing a large golden crown that was three yards high, all set with diamonds and carbuncles. In one hand she had a sceptre, and in the other the imperial orb. Bodyguards were standing in two rows at her sides: each one smaller than the other, beginning with the largest giant and ending with the littlest dwarf, who was no larger than my little finger. Many princes and dukes were standing in front of her.

The man went and stood among them and said, 'Wife, are you emperor now?'

'Yes,' she said, 'I am emperor.'

He stood and looked at her, and after thus looking at her for a while, he said, 'Wife, it is very nice that you are emperor.'

'Husband,' she said. 'Why are you standing there? Now that I am emperor, I want to become the Pope!'

'Oh, wife!' said the man. 'What do you not want? There is only one Pope in all Christendom. He cannot make you Pope! Anyhow, I thought you were C of E!'

'Husband,' she said, 'I want to become Pope. Go there immediately. I must become Pope this very day.'

'Heavens above!' he howled. 'I cannot tell him that! The fish cannot make you Pope!'

'Husband, what nonsense!' said the woman. 'If he can make me emperor, then he can make me Pope as well. It's only logical. Go there immediately. I am emperor, and you are my husband and my subject. Are you going, or are you disobeying?'

The emperor cast a glance over to her executioner, who stepped forward with a large sword.

Then the frightened man went. He felt sick all over and his legs were shaking. The wind was blowing over the land and clouds flew by as the darkness of evening fell. Leaves blew from the trees and the water roared and boiled as it crashed onto the shore. In the distance he could see boats on the river in difficulty as they tossed and turned on the waves. The sky had turned red and the heavy air crackled. Full of despair he stood there and said:

Little Man, Little Man, O hear me!
Big fish, little fish, swimming so free.
My wife, my strife, O hard-nosed Jill,
Wants not, wants not, what I will.

Up popped the Fish Prince, 'What does she want then?' he asked.

'Oh, mercy!' said the man. 'Now she wants to become Pope!'

The fish swished his tail. 'Go home, go home,' said the fish. 'She is already Pope.'

Then he went home and when he arrived there, there was a large church surrounded by nothing but palaces. He forced his way through the crowd. Inside everything was illuminated with thousands and thousands of lights and his wife was clothed in pure gold and sitting on a much higher throne. She was wearing three large golden crowns. She was surrounded with church-like splendour and at her sides there were two banks of candles. The largest was as thick and as tall as the largest tower, down to the smallest kitchen candle. And all the emperors, kings, queens and bishops were kneeling before her kissing her pontiff's slipper.

'Wife,' said the man, giving her a good look, 'are you Pope now?'

'Yes,' she said, 'I am Pope.'

Then he stood there looking at her, and it was as if he were looking into the bright sun. After he had looked at her for a while he said, 'Wife, it is good that you are Pope!'

She stood there as stiff as a tree, neither stirring nor moving.

Then he said, 'Wife, be satisfied now that you are Pope. There is nothing else that you can become.'

'I have to think about that,' said the woman.

Then they both went to bed, but she was not satisfied. Her desires would not let her sleep. She kept thinking about what she wanted to become next.

The man slept well and soundly for he had run about a lot during the day, but the woman could not sleep at all; she tossed and turned from one side to the other all night long, always thinking about what she could become next – but she failed to think of anything.

Then, when the sun was about to rise and she saw the early light of dawn, she sat up in bed and watched through the window as the sun came up.

'Aha!' she thought. 'Could not I cause the sun and the moon to rise?'

'Husband,' she said, poking him in the ribs with her elbow, 'wake up and go back to the fish. I want to become God!'

The man, who was still mostly asleep, was so startled that he fell out of bed. He thought that he had misunderstood her, so, rubbing his eyes, he said, 'Wife, what did you say?'

'Husband,' she said, 'I cannot stand it when I see the sun and the moon rising and I cannot cause them to do so. I will not have a single hour of peace until I myself can cause them to rise.'

She looked at him so gruesomely that he shuddered.

'Go there immediately. I want to become God!'

'Oh, wife,' said the man, falling on his knees before her, 'the fish cannot do that! He can make you emperor and Pope, but I beg you, be satisfied and remain Pope!'

Anger fell over her. Her hair flew wildly about her head. Tearing at her bodice she kicked him with her foot and shouted, 'I cannot stand it! I cannot stand it any longer! Go there immediately; otherwise I'll condemn your soul to eternal punishment!'

He put on his trousers and ran off like a madman.

Outside such a storm was raging that he could hardly stand on his feet. Houses and trees were blowing over. The hills of the Cotswolds were shaking and honey-coloured rocks were rolling from the banks into the river. The sky was as black as pitch; there was thunder and lightning. On the edge of the water he cried:

Little Man, Little Man, O hear me!
Big fish, little fish, swimming so free.
My wife, my strife, O hard-nosed Jill,
Wants not, wants not, what I will.

Up popped the Fish Prince. 'What does she want then?'

'Oh,' he lamented, 'mercy on our souls! She wants to become God.'

The fish swished his tail. 'Go home, go home and you'll see what her wish has brought her. I can give you no more. Goodbye!'

The fisherman returned home, expecting to see the Pope's palace or something even more extravagant. Instead, he was stunned to see the shack they used to live in. He went inside and saw his wife sitting there in rags, for once speechless.

'Ah, home at last!' the fisherman smiled. He joined his wife, sitting down with a sigh.

And they are sitting there even today.

Although this is clearly a Brothers Grimm classic, Katherine M. Briggs notes that 'a lively version [of the tale] was heard in Oxfordshire in 1965.' I have relocated it to Dorchester-on-Thames, with its winding river and many lovely lakes, and have woven in local references, as any teller worth his salt should do. This does not diminish from the original, which readers are encouraged to refer to. Of course, fishing is not permitted without a permit – even if your wife is the Pope!

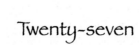

Twenty-seven

THE SKELETON
IN THE CELLAR

Lord Lovell fled the battle. The King had defeated the rebel army at Stoke and he was on the losing side. He narrowly escaped the rout with his life. The armies were cap-a-pie behind him; a seething melee of pikes, swords and bodies. It was turning into a massacre.

The screams of the dying were drowned out by the blood pounding in his ears, the thud of hooves beneath him, as Lovell galloped from the battlefield. Ahead lay the River Trent. At his back were Royalist soldiers. His fate at their hands did not bear thinking about – the Tower; a swift blow from the executioner's axe, if he was lucky. Lovell plunged his horse into the river and it flailed wildly. Underneath his heavy armour it struggled to keep its head above the strong current. It panicked, eyes rolling, legs thrashing. An arrow from the riverbank pierced its neck and, gurgling blood, it sank into the water, cold as death. His lifeless steed started to drag Lovell down as well, his boot caught in the stirrup. Frantically he struggled free, taking his knife to the leather strap. With a grunt he broke free but now the weight of the armour dragged him down. His chest felt like it would burst as he pulled himself free from his metal skin. Then, mercifully, he was able to swim to the surface. He burst into the light, blinking, breath-less – alive, but for how long? He would have been a sitting duck then if not for the river's current, which had pulled him some distance downstream. He appeared among the rushes on the far bank, hidden from his enemy – who saw Lovell's horse floating by and grunted with satisfaction before turning back.

Gasping and spluttering, Lovell pulled himself onto the shore, looking more like a drowned rat than a Lord. Yet he had escaped with his life. He shivered uncontrollably. Being alive was pain-ful! He had to keep moving. Wearily, he dragged himself up and headed on through the woods, providing his flight with merciful cover – the green shadows swallowed him.

After many days of hiding and running, he made it back to Minster Lovell, the family home, ensconced in sylvan splendour next to the Windrush. Here he commanded his servants – who were relieved to see him but terrified of the repercussions – to hide him in a secret room he had installed in the cellar with all that he needed to be comfortable: candles, flint and tinder, a chamber pot, a blanket, a good book, plus pen, ink and paper, to write his account. His faithful servant – a retainer of the family of many years loyal service – was given the key, locking his lord in but agree-ing to bring him food and empty his chamber pot, until Lovell could make good his escape.

The Lord relaxed. It seemed he was safe. He had built the secret vault to be well hidden and nigh on impregnable. The walls were solid stone, the door heavy-beamed and bolted with iron. There was one tiny air vent, but it was well-camouflaged and let in only the faintest suggestion of light.

He passed the time by reading and writing – one day, his account might save his life. He had time to reflect on the events that had led to this 'belly of the whale'. Once, the Lovells had been in the King's favour and granted the fine house with its extensive park-land, which was formerly part of the Royal Forest of Wychwood. During the War of the Roses, the Lovells loyally supported the King and the Lancastrians, but when he succeeded his favour, he turned to York. This seemed to pay off when Richard, Duke of

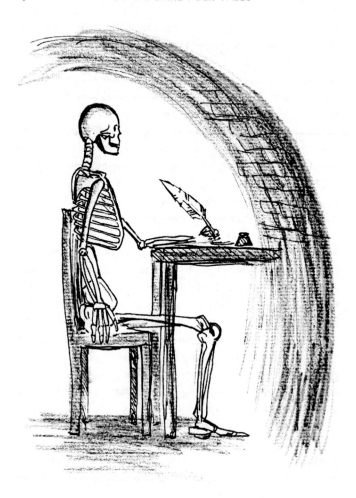

Gloucester, was made king after the murder of his nephews in the Tower of London. Lovell was made viscount and bestowed with further honours: Chief Butler of England. He didn't care about the cruel rhymes the riff-raff shared:

The catte, the ratte and Lovell the dogge
Rylyth all England under the Hogge.

But, it all backfired with the death of the King at the Battle of Bosworth and the crowning of Henry Tudor. Then there was the terrified fleeing to France; the return, two years later, to support a rebellion headed by Lambert Simnel, the Young Pretender; the devastating defeat at Stoke and now here he was – hiding in the cellar of his own house.

Where was that servant? His food had run out hours ago and he was starving! And the place was reeking with his full chamber pot and body odour. He hadn't had a proper wash in days. How low he had fallen, the Chief Butler of England! He called out for his servant, but received no reply.

He called out again and again until his voice was raw.

Desperate hours followed. He paced the room back and forth until he lost the energy. He drank the last of his water and grew weaker still. He licked the walls for moisture but that just made him retch. He slept fitfully and had feverish dreams in which his life played out before him in a grotesque pantomime. Figures from the past came back to mock him. Where had he gone wrong? His last candle guttered out and he was left in darkness, trapped, in his own house: buried alive. With his remaining strength he sat back in his chair.

Years later, in 1708, workmen discovered a secret vault while laying the foundations of a new chimney. Nervously, they knocked out the bricks and thrust a torch into the dark space. They were greeted with a grisly visage. A skeleton sat at a table, on which was placed a book, pen and papers. A decaying cap lay on the floor bearing the Lovell insignia of the hound.

There was a sudden inrush of air and the whole thing turned to dust before their eyes.

What had happened to the faithful servant – had he betrayed his master, or had something else prevented him from returning?

The dead keep their secrets.

We hope.

It is said every family has a skeleton in the attic; in this case it was in the basement. These days, Minster Lovell Hall is a picturesque ruin looked after by English Heritage. Following the defeat of the House of York in the Battle of Bosworth in 1485, the hall passed into the hands of the Crown and eventually, in 1602, into the possession of the successful lawyer Sir Edward Coke. His descendant, Thomas Coke, later Earl of Leicester, was in residence in 1721, and in 1728 he assumed the title Lord Lovell of Minster Lovell. The hall was, however, abandoned in favour of the Cokes' seat at Holkham, Norfolk. The dismantling of the buildings begun in the 1730s, and in about 1747 most of the buildings were dismantled, the east and west ranges and the kitchens being demolished for building stone. Whether it's ghostly resident is finally at rest, who can say? Does Lovell hound his erstwhile servant through the dismal halls of the afterlife?

Twenty-eight

THE STRANGE CASE OF ANNE GREEN

Anne Green was a maid, but no maiden. This was plain to all with eyes to see that morning – green as her maiden name she was; but a maiden no more she was, as her body undeniably told her. She clutched her stomach and groaned, 'I am with child.'

What would befall her? What would befall the child?

She was twenty-two years of age, strong-limbed, fleshy, some would say plain, but that was not enough to deter the grandson of her employer, Sir Thomas Read of Dun Tews, Oxfordshire, from seducing her. For Mr Geoffrey Read, Anne was an easy conquest; a quick fumble in the broom cupboard, an afternoon's distraction, but to Anne the consequences were devastating. Over the coming weeks, as Geoffrey's casual ardour cooled, her body grew hot and she felt strange until finally, one morning, she realised what she had feared and suspected. She carried his child.

But alas, her chores did not relent – down on her knees every day, scrubbing, kneading dough, sweeping, clearing the grates and laying the fires, beating out carpets; the list was endless. Her swelling belly was well-hidden beneath the folds of her uniform, but her body could not lie and one morning she keeled over in pain. She managed to rush to her room without being spotted with

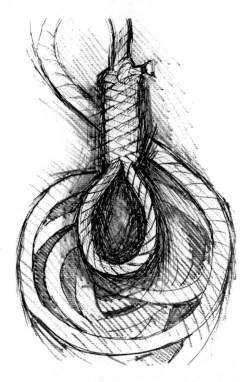

blood trickling down her leg. There, in her small maid's room at the top of the house, on her hard, narrow bed, she gave birth to her child. She stifled her screams to avoid discovery, but when, exhausted, she drew the child to her, she saw a fearful sight. The tiny infant boy was still and silent. Grief-stricken, she hid the little body in a bundle of her dirty linen; but when it was discovered by the other servants there was a great commotion. When they asked her if it was her child she nodded. She was kept in her room until the authorities arrived. There were a lot of questions. Her head swirled. The household watched her leave in cold silence, their terrible stares freezing her. She wanted to protest her innocence but what was the point. Yes, the child was hers and in a way she was to blame; it was punishment for her moment's indiscretion. The Reads glowered down at her, a united front. Geoffrey could not look her in the eye.

Anne was taken into custody and placed in a cold cell in Oxford Gaol. There she waited for three weeks, with no word of explanation, until the next sessions were held in the city. She was brought before the judge and found guilty of the murder of an innocent child and sentenced to death. No one came forward to defend her, certainly not the Reads. She was a poor maidservant, of lowly origin. What chance did she have of justice? On Saturday, 14th of December 1650, she was taken from her cell to the county gallows in the cattle yard in Oxford – where a great crowd had gathered. Her hands were tied behind her back and she wore a simple woollen shift. Her hair was down and she wished they would let her brush it. There was a light frost on the ground, scattered with steaming dung and bright red berries. The trees were skeletal hands, held up, placatingly to the iron sky. Her breath froze before her in white clouds. She experienced it as though in a waking dream – as though it was happening to someone else. In grim silence Anne was led to the gallows, where a robed priest and a cloaked hangman awaited. A psalm was sung, the melody sending her into a trance. Someone spoke up – a friend, one of the servants – against the Reads, for whom she had worked so loyally; who had used her so ill. There were murmurs of anger in the crowd. Others shouted 'hang her'.

She was led to the ladder. Her knees trembled and she nearly stumbled, but the hangman kindly gave her his hand, massive, rough and firm. Anne gazed out over the solemn crowd. Why was this happening to her? She saw the sorrow in their faces and wanted to tell them not to mind for her. She would soon be with her boy and beyond all suffering. Before she could speak, a hood was placed over her head and all was hot darkness. There was only her breathing, but even that grew restricted as she felt a noose being tightened about her neck. Then, the ladder was kicked away. She flailed. White pain flared in her brain, convulsed through her body. It was as though the tap of life had been turned off.

She hung for half an hour, during which time some of her friends thumped her on the breast, 'others hanging with all their weight upon her legs,' as it was described afterwards, 'sometimes lifting her up, and then pulling her down again with a sudden jerk, thereby the sooner to despatch her out of her pain.' At this point the Under Sheriff required them to desist, lest they should break the rope. When everyone thought she was dead, the body was taken down and put in a coffin and carried to the private house where Dr William Petty, a reader in anatomy at Oxford, lodged. He and his colleague, Thomas Willis, were delighted with this fresh corpse to study and made ready to conduct an autopsy.

There, a true wonder took place.

When the coffin was opened, the poor broken body of Anne was observed to make a breath and a rattle was heard in her throat. William Petty and Thomas Willis, his colleague, abandoned all thoughts of a dissection and proceeded to revive their patient. They held her up in the coffin and then, wrenching open her teeth, they poured some hot cordial into her mouth, which caused her to cough more. They then rubbed and chafed her fingers, hands, arms and feet, and, after a quarter of an hour of this, poured more cordial into her mouth and tickled her throat with a feather; she opened her eyes momentarily.

What must she have thought at this moment – these two gentle-men leaning over her, attending to her every need and comfort? Their accents and manners were so refined, the clothes and lodg-ings so elegant. Was she in some kind of strange heaven?

What they did next perhaps dispelled that illusion. The doctors opened a vein and bled Anne of five ounces of blood; they then continued administering the cordial and rubbing her arms and legs. Compressing bandages were applied to her limbs. Heating plasters were put to her chest and another was apparently inserted as an enema, 'to give heat and warmth to her bowels.' They then placed her in a warm bed with another woman, to lie with her and keep her warm for she truly looked like death warmed up.

After twelve hours she began to speak and twenty-four hours after her revival, she was answering questions freely. After two days her memory was normal – apart from the period of the execution and the resuscitation. At four days she was eating solid food and, one month after the event, she was fully recovered – except for the period of amnesia that had been noted at two weeks. There were frequent observations of the state of the pulse; her colour was observed closely; and soon after her revival her face was noted to be sweating, swelling, and very red – particularly near the place where the knot of the rope had been fastened. There were frequent tests of her sight and her hearing and also of her understanding of questions. Even when she was mute, she was asked to move her hand or open an eye if she could hear the question. Her memory was frequently tested by specific questions. When her memory returned after two days, the following description was made: 'Her memory was like a clock whose weights had been taken off a while and afterwards hung on again.' At two weeks there was the interesting observation of the slight return of her memory of the execution. She remembered 'a fellow in a blanket', who could only have been the executioner in his cloak. What she had seen beyond the veil, if anything, she kept to herself – but there was a strange light in her eyes and a certain feyness in her manner. Some remarked that there was a spiritual light about her. Indeed, some thought her now holy and certainly innocent of her former crime.

The Under Sheriff of Oxford solicited the governor of Oxford Gaol and the Justices of the Peace for her reprieve. The Justices decided that the hand of God had preserved her and they wished to co-operate with divine providence in granting her a reprieve, pending the time that a pardon might be obtained – which was subsequently granted. Many people in Oxford had seen her during her recovery and it seems that her father charged for admission. This collection and a subsequent financial appeal on her behalf produced many pounds, which paid the bill of the apothecary, her food and lodging, and the legal expenses of her pardon.

Anne Green's fame continued after her full recovery when she returned to some friends in the country, taking with her the coffin in which she had lain. Yet her famous execution and resuscitation was more than a Nine-day Wonder. Life continued and, it seemed, even a heart can recover and find love again.

Anne met a man who treated her well. She married, bore him three children and lived for a full fifteen years beyond her 'death'.

What did Anne see on the 'other side'? Did her memory ever return? If it did, she kept the secrets of the grave with her up until she met the Grim Reaper a second time.

The strange case of Anne Green, regarded as a sure sign of the hand of God acting on behalf of the innocent, was recorded in a broadside ballad and popular pamphlets. The most notable of these was published in 1651: 'Newes from the Dead, or a True and Exact Narration of the Miraculous Deliverance of Anne Greene ... written by a Scholler in Oxford ... whereunto are prefixed certain Poems casually written upon that subject.' The twenty-five poems include a set of Latin verses by no less than Christopher Wren. And so, from her lowly circumstances, Anne Green's name was raised aloft by the likes of the architect of St Paul's Cathedral and preserved in posterity.

William Petty and Thomas Willis also achieved considerable fame for their conduct in the case. Petty left the practice of medicine shortly after; but Willis went on to become an Oxford professor and then a wealthy London physician.

Of the Reads and the Judge, no more is said.

Twenty-nine

THE HEADLESS
STEPSON

When Sir Robert Pye of Faringdon House remarried, his new wife took an immediate disliking to Hampden – Sir Robert's son from his previous marriage. Whatever he did it could not please her, and she used her influence to turn Sir Robert's opinion against him also. Slowly, stealthily, she poisoned her husband's heart against his own son. He was a good-for-nothing wastrel. What did he do with his wealth, his privileges? Nothing! He liked to idle his days in the local taverns – whoring and gambling and drinking. Surely Sir

Robert deserved a more fitting heir? So, when Lady Pye found herself pregnant it seemed fate had smiled. There was only one thing
in the way of her only flesh and blood inheriting Faringdon House
and Sir Robert's fortune – Hampden Pye.

With this new babe on the scene, Hampden's life was becoming unbearable – and not because of a wailing baby in the house.
His stepmother watched him like a hawk and controlled his comings and goings. This drove him from the stifling atmosphere of
the house and back to the local taverns, again and again. Soon
he found solace in a particularly charming barmaid. When he
announced he was going to marry her, his parents were horrified.
Did this not confirm how wayward their son had become? He had
allowed a local slut to inveigle herself into his heart – attracted by
the strong aphrodisiac of wealth, their wealth! If she bore him a
son … it didn't bear thinking about. Something had to be done!

Lady Pye took matters in hand. She arranged for her stepson
to be shanghaied onto a Naval ship. While he was out drinking
in the local tavern, a press-gang came in. They dropped the King's
Shilling in his tankard while he was relieving himself outside.
When he returned to finish his ale, he discovered the coin in the
bottom and knew what it meant. Suddenly, there was a group of
mean-looking thugs in front of him. He waved a purse in their
faces but they roughly dragged him out of the tavern and bundled
him into a carriage. He was tied-up and taken apace all the way
to Plymouth.

There a ship was waiting, about to sail to the Iberian peninsula.
It was captained by Sir George Rooke, whom Lady Pye had bribed
with her gold to 'take care' of her stepson. Sir Robert had been
persuaded by Lady Pye that it would be in his son's best interests to
join the Navy. He would no doubt be posted overseas and would
be safely out of reach of the gold-digging barmaid. This seemed
like a severe but necessary measure. His son needed to sober up
and see sense – a blast of sea air and Navy life might be just the
ticket to put him on the straight and narrow.

A bucket of icy seawater shocked Hampden awake. Spluttering,
he stood up, or tried to. The ground was unsteady beneath his feet.

The men around him laughed – a rum-looking bunch, sailors of the English Navy. He was on a ship of the Fleet. Sir George Rooke introduced himself. 'You are on your way to the Spanish main, Hampden Pye. Time to sober up and get shipshape! Put a uniform on man. You're in the King's Navy now!'

When he had gotten over his sudden and dramatic change in circumstance, Hampden Pye took to life at sea like a duck to water. When their vessel engaged the enemy in battle, Hampden Pye was right there, on the foeman's deck, sword in hand, the first man on board. Bullets flying about him, he never felt more alive.

Yet in the fog of war, all manner of things can happen.

In the middle of a battle, Hampden was pushed in front of a canon by 'Hairy-faced Dick' and his head was blown clean off.

Back in Faringdon, the news was received by Lady Pye with what seemed genuine shock. She publicly displayed her grief, organising a memorial service in Hampden's honour at Faringdon church; with it she hoped to lay the final obstacle of her plan to rest.

Triumphantly, she climbed into her coach and four, and as it drew away from the church she breathed a sigh of relief. Then she felt an icy presence in the carriage. Although she rode alone – the footman outside – she sensed another in the carriage with her, in the shadows on the opposite side; a figure of a man in Naval uniform. He was resting something on his knee. He leant forward, showing her the severed stump of his neck. Then he lifted up his head. The face of her stepson looked at her and smiled.

Her screams could be heard throughout the village, but the servants could see nothing and were quite concerned for the lady's sanity. She was taken swiftly back to Faringdon House and was told to rest by her physician. Clearly the strain of her recent loss had been too much.

The servants were told that Lady Pye must be given plenty of peace and privacy – the very thing she did not need. She could never be alone! And she never was – she always had company. In hall or in bower, wherever the place, whatever the hour, Lady Pye muttered and talked to the air. Once, her servants found her, her eyes fixed on an empty chair.

Her young son showed little concern for his mother's deteriorating health and erratic behaviour. He was more interested in the thousand pounds a year he was now due.

It was not until he too saw his stepbrother appear and he ran gibbering to his mother, that she was forced to reveal her wicked deed.

The headless ghost of Hampden also terrorised his old Captain at his club in Bath, where he had retired as an Admiral. As grey as a badger and as thin as a rake, Sir George Rooke always seemed to be looking over his shoulder, flinching at this and that. He would frequently go to the Assembly Rooms hoping to lose himself in playing cards, until his knaves stood upside down and the Jack of Clubs frowned at him. Then the kings, aces and best trumps started cavorting with the queens. Then he would look up and see Hampden Pye, counting the tricks with his head on his knees.

Hairy-faced Dick did not escape either. In Ratcliffe Highway, Hairy-faced Dick had set himself up with his Navy pension an old marine store full of rusty locks and dusty bags, musty phials and fusty rags. A great black doll hung over the door – but this could not keep a vengeful ghost away. The first to see it was Thirsty Nan, his lusty old woman who liked the sauce. She blinked and stared into the gloom of the store, calling 'Who's there?' Out of the shadows came the headless ghost. She wailed and dropped her rum with a smash, running howling back to Hairy-faced Dick. 'What is it woman? Stop your wail…' The words stuck in his gullet – the pipe dropped from his lips. He went pale and fell to his knees as the shadow of a sabre fell across his terrified face. Thirsty Nan screamed and all went silent.

Hampden's headless phantom haunted the graveyard of Faringdon church, where his memorial service had been held. His restless spirit worried the good folk of Faringdon for a hundred years before they were eventually forced to have the local vicar exorcise him – using a bell, book and candle. And so, in the early nineteenth century, Hampden Pye finally found peace, and so did the descendants of Sir Robert Pye – the former head of the household.

The Pye legacy has lived on, not only in a ballad – 'The Legend of Hamilton Tighe' made famous in The Ingoldsby Legends – but also in a nursery rhyme. Legend also has it that the Poet Laureate, Henry James Pye (the twentieth-century British historian Lord Blake called Pye 'the worst Poet Laureate in English history, with the possible exception of Alfred Austin') traipsed up the hill each day with a sapling or seedling of Scots Pine. Because of this it became known as Pye's Folly and, in due course, Folly Hill. Before that it was known as Cromwell's Battery; and later Lord Berners' Folly. Henry James Pye (renowned for his tedious poetry – indeed, Pye's successor, Robert Southey, wrote in 1814: 'I have been rhyming as doggedly and dully as if my name had been Henry James Pye') his work on Folly Hill has been described as the most poetic act of his life. His critics lampooned him in the nursery rhyme 'Sing a song of sixpence, a pocketful of rye – four and twenty blackbirds baked in a Pye…' To this day, Faringdon house is famous for its dyed pigeons, one of the many eccentric customs of Lord Berners, who built Faringdon Folly on Folly Hill in 1935 (as a twenty-first birthday present). Renowned for his comic attitude to life, Lord Berners put a notice above the door of the tower saying: 'Members of the public committing suicide from this tower do so at their own risk'. Around the town one can see a number of stone plaques with comments such as 'Please do not throw stones at this notice', reflecting Lord Berners' ongoing influence on the town.

Thirty

THE GHOST OF
CRAKE'S SCHOOL

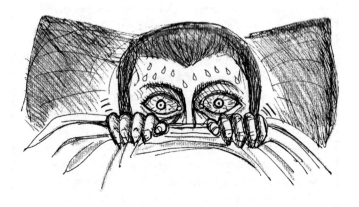

It was always at bedtime she would appear, just as you was tucked
up nice in bed with the other boys in the dorm – the old stables
and coach house which never seemed to warm up. Just after the
lights had gone out and everyone had finally settled down – after
a period of silence punctuated only by the steady breathing of the
boys – would the soft footsteps be heard. They would come out of
the lonely room on the top floor, go along the passage and down
those damned creaking stairs. A chilling presence would enter

their room, floating among the beds as the boys lay frozen in their bunks. Finally, mercifully, it would leave.

Many of the older boys had anecdotes of doors opening and slamming of their own accord. Door handles had been seen to move on their own and noises could be heard throughout the building, as if things were being picked up and dropped when no one was there.

One of them swore blind he actually saw her. He was a fey sort, of Irish blood; prone to superstition the cynical ones said; others said that he had the 'Sight'. Wild-eyed and gibbering, he described her to his schoolmates, who gathered around, pale faced, huddled in blankets. 'She was wearing a black flowing cloak with a purple ribbon in her auburn hair. She looked sad.'

It was 1854 at Crake's School, formerly Courtiers House – a red brick Georgian mansion. It had been purchased in 1846 for a low rent; the building had been in a sorrowful state. The master took no heed to the stories of the ghost, but this would explain why it was only twenty pounds per annum. Every pupil there knew the story of the ghost. They were told it – whether they liked it or not, on their first night in the dorms by older boys who delighted in the terror it induced.

Her name was Sarah Fletcher, they whispered, like some kind of invocation of evil.

On the 7th of June 1799, twenty-nine-year-old Mrs Sarah Fletcher committed suicide at Courtiers – as back then it was her marital home. She hung herself from the curtain rails of her four-poster bed using a handkerchief and a piece of cord.

It is said that she was driven to take her own life after she discovered her husband, who was a Captain in the Royal Navy, was arranging a bigamous marriage to a wealthy heiress. This she heard after she had received word that he had 'died at sea'. When she got wind of this, Sarah went to the church and actually stopped the wedding from taking place – like a 'mad woman' she was, the shocked guests had agreed, beside herself with rage and grief. The congregation looked at her with disgust, as though *she* was in the wrong.

And yet the Captain knew he had transgressed. The guilt flickered in his eyes as Sarah was dragged kicking and screaming away – like a witch being cast out of God's house.

Following this, Captain Fletcher returned to sea – but the betrayal and neglect was too much for Sarah to bear. By the time she hung herself, her husband was said to be en-route to the East Indies.

There was a tribunal and the jury, without hesitation, announced the verdict of lunacy.

Normally, a lot of cackling and howling follows this – much to the abject terror of the new intake, saucer-eyed behind the sheets.

What of poor Sarah? She is buried in the Abbey Church of St Peter and St Paul, Dorchester-on-Thames. Her epitaph reads:

'May her Soul meet that Peace in Heaven which this Earth has denied her.'

The school, which was a private academy, opened in 1846 and was referred to as Crake's School after its master. Around 1854, the children were amongst those who witnessed the haunting. Later, in the 1850s, it became a commercial school which had thirty pupils. By 1866, it was referred to as a grammar school. The school moved from Courtiers in 1868, after a fever outbreak in Clifton Hampden. Maude Ffoulkes mentions the haunting in True Ghost Stories *(1936), which she co-authored with Marchioness Townsend. Jessie Middleton quotes Ffoulkes in her account of the story 'Sarah Fletcher'. Ffoulkes visited Courtiers House in the early twentieth century, when it was a girl's institution, and wrote a pamphlet called 'The Story of Sarah Fletcher' (1913) after looking into the haunting. It included testimonies from Revd Poyntz, minister of Abbey*

Church at the time; and Revd Edward Crake, who had lived at Courtiers as a child. When the school closed it was divided up into cottages and then eventually became an institution for girls. What was heartbreaking was the reaction to Sarah's suicide. Jacksons Oxford Journal *for Saturday, 15th June 1799, stated: 'the derangement of her mind appearing very evident, as well as from many other circumstances, the jury, without hesitation, found the verdict – Lunacy'.*

May the ghost of Sarah Fletcher be placated by the telling of her story and the injustice she received.

Thirty-one

THE LEGEND OF ST FREMUND

King Offa of Mercia had a son called Fremund, who he had high hopes for – as the Crown Prince, one day the kingdom would be his. But Fremund was a strong-willed boy and when it reached the time when he needed to shoulder some responsibility, he fled. Royal life had always been cloying for him – there was something about the endless feasting and finery that just didn't agree with him. He preferred his own company; prayer; or walking in nature. He was sick at heart of the bloodthirsty times he lived in. The Law of the Sword did not appeal to him as much as the Word of the Lord.

One day, he decided to give it all up. He set sail with twelve companions, brothers and kindred spirits, in a birlinn from Caerleon-on-Usk, eventually landing at 'llefaye' – a small rocky island in the mouth of the Severn which was home to a colony of puffins and little else. It had a harsh beauty of its own and it suited his temperament. Here he established a hermitage and began a simple, devout life.

On the other side of the isle of Britain, things were not so tranquil. Viking invaders had swept across East Anglia, martyring King Edmund. The Mercian people were headless – for King Offa had died – and so, in desperation, a group were sent in search of the lost prince. It was Mercia's darkest hour and a leader was needed.

The emissaries found Fremund upon the small island, leading a peaceful, contemplative life. They pleaded with him to return. Why should he? Well, it was his own people, his own land. If he had any honour, how could he forsake it? And so, finally, he accepted. He had put aside the sword – but now he had to seize it and become a leader. Steeling himself, he put aside his monk's robes and put on his armour. Leaving his pilgrim staff on the island, as they put out in a small boat for the mainland, he unsheathed the sword and held it aloft in the morning light.

In haste and secrecy, they returned to Mercia.

Fremund, son of Offa, rallied his people and led them in a victorious battle at Radford Semele. His father would have been proud of his heir.

Alas, as Fremund knelt in prayer to give thanks for his victory, one of his own men struck off his head. Some say he was envious, but perhaps other forces influenced him – was he a turncoat; a Viking assassin; or had Old Nick himself possessed him?

As his followers looked on, aghast at the tragedy, something astonishing happened. Fremund's headless corpse twitched into life, blood still flowing from the gaping wound of the neck. The body stood up and picked its head and began to walk. The onlookers were too stunned to react, they could only follow as the headless Fremund walked and walked – until he eventually stopped between Harbury and Whitton. From beneath his very feet a well sprang up, flowing with good, clean water. Fremund then began to wash his own head, cleaning it of the blood from battle. When he had finished, a sigh escaped his ruined corpse and he finally lay down and died.

When his followers recovered from witnessing this miracle, Fremund's remains were taken to the church of Offchurch in Warwickshire. This became a shrine for all those wanting healing. In AD 93, the relics were taken to Cropredy in Oxfordshire. Here they remained, in a chapel, until the thirteenth century, when they were once more moved to Dunstable. Yet Cropredy, having been

so long associated with the saint, retained its sanctity and importance as a place of pilgrimage. It was only during the Civil War that his shrine was destroyed by Cromwell's army.

No sign of the shrine remains, but Fremund's spirit perhaps still lingers in the village of the stream by the hill.

The village has become a modern place of pilgrimage, as every year thousands of folk music fans gather for the annual Cropredy Festival – the Fairport Convention reunion. For over forty years – since the band formed in 1967 – friends have gathered here, and to mark four decades of association with the village the band paid for a Festival Bell to be cast, which

now hangs in the local church, calling new worshippers to this
little village in the northernmost tip of Oxfordshire. Perhaps St
Fremund would have approved – his head swaying like the bell
in time to the music of the life.

Thirty-two

YOUNG ALFRED, SON OF WANTAGE

Sometimes, the littlest things can become the greatest.

Alfred was the youngest son of Aethelwulf and his wife, Osberga. He was born at the Royal Palace of Wantage in AD 849. The older folk called it Gwynedd-iog, or 'White Hills Place' – after the chalk downs that rose to the South. Yet the old tongue was discouraged. A new tide was sweeping the land, forged in the clash between the Cross and the Hammer.

It was a dangerous world for a small boy to grow up in, but the young prince – oblivious to the turmoil beyond the walls of White Hills Place – found it exciting. His local landscape seemed carved for adventure.

Alfred's hometown had once been the place of two rivers but one had faded away, so it was referred to as 'waning river' in the common Saxon tongue and, over time, it became known as Wantage. Young Alfred pondered whether one river had subsumed the other, or if they had mingled together – it was hard to tell, as he gazed into the waters of Letcombe Brook one day. He reflected how King Arthur had fought against Alfred's own people when they were considered the invaders, and yet here they were, fighting off the new wave – the Danelaw Vikings – sweeping in from the East. Withstanding

this were the white hills of Wantage: here his father's shining palace stood like a pale sword against the night – a Saxon Minster; home of a long line of kings, of which Alfred was descended.

Alfred wondered where Aetheldred was. They were due at the feast and his brother was always late for things! Yet he loved his older brother; growing up they had been inseparable; but Alfred sensed a change in Aetheldred these days – moping about or restless, as though waiting for something, something that would change their lives forever.

The wyrd had singled out a special fate for both of them. Their father had instilled into them this noble destiny, saying they were descended from the old gods – Woden, Sceaf and Geat. He would insist they honoured them in their prayers in the groves and by the river. Their ancestors had brought these gods with them to these lands and now this land was theirs. Alfred felt closest to them at a spring he liked to bathe in on the edge of the settlement. Here, he communed with the water spirits. He felt safe – in the water nothing could touch him.

He would remember that feeling in years to come.

Alfred saw little of his father – a King is always busy – and was brought up and educated by his mother. Once, she had promised an expensive illuminated book to the first of her children to learn it by heart. Despite his young age – he was only five at the time – Alfred committed it to memory and won the prize. He treasured that book and loved looking through its colourful pictures, telling stories of kings from long ago. He grew to love all books and the gathering of knowledge. You could learn from the past – it helped you prepare for the future, yet some things are unseen.

When Alfred was sixteen, his father died. It was AD 865 and his older brother, Aethelred, became King of Wessex. The funeral was befitting a king, as was the coronation. Alfred stood by his brother's side – pride mixed with grief.

The wheel turned.

The young prince grew into his body. His limbs lengthened and hardened; his skill with sword and spear improved. No one could catch him on horseback – it was as though he was one with the animal – but faster still were his wits. He honed these like a sword – he had a kingdom to defend.

Alfred quickly became a seasoned warrior and his brother's right-hand man during one of the worst periods of invasion in English history.

The Vikings had been raiding along the English coast for thirty years, but in Aethelred's coronation year they conquered the Kingdom of East Anglia.

Within five years, their Great Heathen Army had arrived in Wessex and seized the Royal palace at Reading, in Berkshire. The local ealdorman managed to contain them until the King arrived with Alfred and the English army. The attempted siege at Reading was unsuccessful.

Soon afterward, in January AD 871, Alfred regrouped his brother's troops on the nearby Berkshire Downs. Riding to the

top of Blowingstone Hill, Alfred made use of an ancient perforated sarsen stone; known as the 'Blowing Stone', it was capable
of producing a loud, booming sound when blown into correctly.
With the signal sent out across the downs, he rode to a hill-fort
near Ashdown House to gather his men; while Aethelred's men
rallied at nearby Hardwell Camp. Uniting their forces, Aethelred
and Alfred learned that the Danes had encamped at nearby
Uffington Castle.

Alfred's men gathered at the castle that now bears his name in
the parish of Ashbury. Aethelred's troops had taken up position
not far away at Hardwell Camp (these days known as Compton
Beauchamp). Meanwhile, the Danes had reached Uffington
Castle, where they settled down for the night.

On the morning of the 8th of January 871, the two sides met
on the plain known as 'Aschendune', or Ashdown, where a single
stunted thorn tree grew. Alfred pondered this tree. It reminded
him of the World Ash – Yggdrasil. He took it as a good omen.
Whoever took this field of battle would win the war. The King
prayed quietly to the old gods for victory.

Then a horn blast split the air. It was beginning.

They drew up their troops in two columns each. The Danish
divisions were commanded by their Kings, Bagsecg and Halfdan,
and five Earls; the English by Aethelred and Alfred. There they
waited, jeering and shouting at one another. Alfred was keen to
get to grips with the enemy; but Aethelred decided to spend the
ensuing lull in prayer for victory. He left the battlefield for the little
church at Aston, and, despite Alfred's insistence, he would not
return until the priest had finished. Ever afterwards he was known
as Aethelred the Unready.

So the young Prince had to make a decision: should he wait for
his brother or fight the battle without him? He could not keep his
troops on edge for long. The Danes had already deployed themselves on the higher ground and to let them charge first would
mean certain defeat. So, despite his brother's orders to the contrary, Alfred rode forth and gave the cry for his own men to attack
first and for the battle to begin.

Never had the white hills seen such carnage and – if the God's were merciful – never would they again. The chalk scars were speckled with blood; the green sward crimson. The bravery of the English warriors overcame all disadvantages and after a long and arduous conflict the invaders were no longer able to withstand the Saxon attacks. They were chased from the field across the meadows to Whistley Marsh – where their previous conflict had ended. Thousands of bodies covered the plain; amongst them was King Bagsecg and the five Danish Earls. The remnants of the Danish army fled the field and returned to Reading.

Victory was Alfred's. He staggered to the lone, gnarled thorn tree, plunged his crimson-stained sword into the soil, and dropped to his knees, giving thanks of the old gods. Yet in that moment he knew they were cruel and bloodthirsty. There had to be another way. The light glinted off of the hilt of his sword. The Cross, rather than the Hammer… Alfred stood, and turned to greet his cheering men – raising his sword aloft by the blade. These were his. This victory was his. This was his day, his hour. It was one of his greatest victories.

But the wheel turns; the tides of wyrd ebb and flow.

A number of defeats followed that same year, resulting in Aethelred's death.

Two rivers … one waned, as the other rose.

The tide of war did not give him time to mourn his brother. In AD 872, after a string of defeats, Alfred made peace with the Danes and within a year Alfred was made King of Wessex.

When the Witan met in the Palace in AD 995, Alfred drew up the 'Wantage Code' of laws and the old and news ways blended.

With unflinching determination, Alfred forged his legend – a great war-chief; but also a devout Christian and a law-maker. Living only fifty years, the young prince from Wantage made his mark on English history, leaving a considerable legacy. Ever afterwards he was known as Alfred the Great – the Saxon exemplar of Englishness; the hero of schoolboys; and, as the champion of the English language, the founder of a nation.

Alfred's birthplace, Wantage, ironically became a lawless place. The traditional trades of Wantage men were largely concerned with the manufacture of hemp, sacking, hats and tallow, as well as tanning. This last industry is remembered by the sheep's knucklebones, still seen to be used as paving in the courtyard of Stiles' Almshouses. However, despite the hard work of some, in the eighteenth century Wantage was famous throughout the land as 'Black Wantage', the home of layabouts and criminals. It was always said that if a prisoner escaped from the Bow Street Runners in London, they would know to search for their prey in Wantage. Such a reputation sprang from the town being a centre for gypsies, pedlars and hawkers, as well as some vagrants – the usual suspects. In those days, gambling was the favourite pastime of the people of Wantage, particularly around cock-fights and badger-baits. There was frequent bull-baiting at the Camel Inn and this is remembered by the name of the 'Bull Ring' in the marketplace. The town was eventually 'cleaned up', and when county borders shifted in 1974 it became part of Oxfordshire. Alfred's statue stands in the town's market place – a symbol of the greatness that man can rise to.

Perhaps he will inspire future sons and daughters of England to do the same.

Thirty-three

THE
BLOWING STONE

Today was a special day. It was Tom's tenth birthday and on your birthday a wish would come true – so his father once told him. Well, Tom only had one wish – not for a bicycle, or a cricket bat, or for a book about King Arthur and his knights – yet he did not want to risk losing its magic, by saying it aloud, even to the wind, as he raced along on that sunny morning, swinging his satchel. If he was quick, he could visit his special place before school. He passed the workmen and gave them a wave: they had been working on the war memorial for the last few weeks and it was nearly done.

Tom loved where he lived. Kingston Lisle, a tiny village in the Vale of the White Horse – 'between horse and smith and stone', as Lob, the old tramp who lived in the woods, would mutter to himself.

Tom felt he had a whole kingdom to play in: the white track of the Ridgeway; the bright horse upon Uffington Hill, carved in elegant curves; Dragon Hill below it, still scorched from the dragon's blood spilled there when Saint George slew it; further along, the creepy barrow of Wayland's Smithy, where he didn't like to linger too long; but best of all, down Blowingstone Hill, tucked away in Martha's garden, the Blowing Stone. It had been the centre of his world as long as he could remember – the schoolteacher had called it an 'omphalos'. He just knew it reassured him to see it there every day – a solid, steady presence. One that didn't leave.

Yet, according to Lob, it had been 'stolen from the hill' by a blacksmith who set it up outside his smithy, which eventually became the village inn. Good for trade, apparently, 'but not for my roses!' complained Martha, fed up of drunken visitors traipsing through her flowerbeds to have a peek at it in her garden.

It had thrilled him since first he had been told the legend of the Blowing Stone, which now seemed as much a part of his world as the old trees that lined the lanes; as his baby brother and sister; as his mother. He had measured his growth against it and now, at ten, he was a good foot higher than it. He would come here after school or when he needed to think – Martha was a friend of the family and didn't mind the young 'un sitting in the garden. He would run his hands over its uneven surface – riddled with holes, like a 'Swiss cheese' apparently, though he had never seen one. Sometimes Tom felt like that stone. The teacher called the grey boulder a 'sarsen', the same as those at Avebury, but a smaller cousin to those mighty giants who danced in a ring.

But best of all, it was said that with the right technique a sound could be produced from it – like a horn blowing. According to the legend, King Alfred (a son of Wantage, where sometimes Tom's Mum would go for market day) used the Blowing Stone to summon his Saxon troops, in readiness for the nearby Battle of Ashdown, against the Vikings who he defeated at Roughthorn Farm (and where his best friend Bert had famously found 'a horn from a Viking helmet'). This was why Tom's village was name Kingston, explained Bert, who, after reading a dusty old book, was now an expert on the matter.

If it was done loud enough to be heard from Uffington Hill, six miles yonder, the blower would be the future King of England. Local children believed it would summon the old king under the hill, if done right under the light of a full moon.

Tom had a different wish, a silent one: to bring his father home. Since he went to fight the Hun in the trenches Dad had not come back. More than anything in the world he wanted him back. He'd seemed like a king to Tom when last he saw him – three years ago, dressed in his uniform, about to set off to 'the Front'. His boots shone nearly as bright as his buttons on that morning, as he wavered on the doorstep in the new sun. He picked Tom up and gave him a final hug, his moustache tickling him as always. Kissing the top of his head, his father set him down and ruffled his hair, smiled sadly at his wife and turned to walk down the path, his kit-bag slung over his shoulder. At the garden gate, he turned a final time and waved.

Then he was gone.

Tom had tried more times than he could remember to produce a sound from that stone and had accomplished nothing more than blowing raspberries. When he shouted into it, it made his voice sound funny, but Martha got fed up of the racket – too many had tried the same thing. But today he felt different – taller and stronger somehow. It was his birthday and now he was ten. He had lived a whole decade! He puffed out his chest, and tested his soft biceps; his body was filling out, but he wasn't as tough as the stone, yet.

He visited Martha's garden often to talk to his father, although he was a little embarrassed about it, so he kept the fact to himself.

He knew his Dad would want to wish him a happy birthday and hear about all his future plans, now that he was a young man. 'My, how you're grown!' he imagined him saying. 'You're a big lad now. The man of the family. Look after Mother, and your brother and sister. Be good. And don't forget your old Dad.'

Tom brushed the tear from his cheek, stood up, took a deep breath and blew.

For the first time, a long, low note was produced, that carried, carried far up Blowingstone Hill, along the Ridgeway, to the White Horse and the Smithy; an echo, carried on the wind, slowing, fading.

Tom stopped and gasped for breath. His heart raced. His skin prickled. Something had happened. He had done it! Then, in the distance, up the lane, he heard the jangling of a harness, the clip-clop of horse hooves on cobbles and the snort of a powerful war-horse.

The King, the King was coming!

Tom raced out into the lane, trembling with excitement, his eyes fixed on the green tunnel of trees and the sun-dappled shadows. There, a figure moving – catching the light, between horse and smith and stone…

His father was coming home.

This story was inspired by the Blowing Stone in Kingston Lisle, weaving the folklore associated with it into a narrative. According to legend, the stone – a 4ft high perforated sarsen – was the means whereby the future King Alfred (originally from Wantage) summoned his Saxon troops in readiness for the nearby Battle of Ashdown against the Vikings. This legend reputedly gives rise to the village's name, 'King's stone', with the Lisle suffix being a later addition. Also, according to legend, a person who is capable of making the Blowing Stone sound a note which

is audible atop Uffington White Horse Hill (where Victorian antiquarians thought King Alfred's troops had camped) will be a future King of England. A deep note can be produced with some persistence. The parish smith brought the stone down into the valley, probably sometime in the early eighteenth century, and set it up adjoining his smithy. By 1809, this building had become the 'Blowing Stone Inn' and the landlord entertained his customers by blowing the stone – for a small price. A second inn of this name now exists in the village of Kingston Lisle.

Thirty-four

THE KING UNDER THE HILL

Scutchamer Knob has always been an uncanny place – a moot for ghosts, a place of old sorcery. Hidden within a small copse next to the ancient Ridgeway, running by the parish of East Hendred, it stands: an earthen mound, a burial mound – some say of the Saxon King, Cwichelm. Long has it been believed that the King under the Hill lives there still, waiting to rise up once more…

Despite his 'lordship-in-residence' – as locals would refer to the Barrow King, doffing their cap to the Knob ('because you never know') – a market would take place there once a year. It was a crossing way which was handy for many a traveller along the high roads. This was a chance to share news and views; barter and trade; woo and box; purchase charms and shoe horses; and pass on the luck. Some, though, like to keep the luck to themselves.

That lot over at East Ilsley weren't happy about that market at the Knob. Since they were granted their charter in 1620 for their own fair, they've acted all high and mighty and petitioned to have the Barrow Fair put down. And that was that. The hill fell silent.

But still some met there by moonlight – for a different kind of market: a market of magic. There, by flickering campfires, the old tales would be brought out and polished up with a bit of breath and shirt-cuff. The old way-tellers, as gnarled as blackthorn cudgels, would spin you a yarn for a quart of ale, or a thumb of baccy.

They would talk of the King under the Hill. How he once strode the land, tall and proud in his shining arm-torcs, buckles and scabbards – one of the Kings of Wessex. How he fought off those Raiders of the North many a time. Here, right here, on this very spot, he stood his ground. There was a prophecy that if the enemy ever made it up the hill, they would never take a ship from England again. And so, when the Danes struggled uphill to camp here in 1006, Cwichelm and his men killed them – every one – stone dead. The good green grass ran red, red, red with blood. Cwichelm wiped his sword with the hem of his cloak and smiled a grim smile; more carrion for the Crow-father.

In his life he had slain many men. In 614, at the Battle of Beandun, did he not slay two thousand and forty-six of the Strangers-beyond-the-Dyke – fighting side-by-side with his fellow King of Wessex, Cynegils? Together they fought King Penda at Cirencester. Those were the glory days. Nothing could stop them when their swords were drawn as one.

Other times were less than glorious, like when he attempted the assassination of King Edwin of Deira. The cut-throat's way

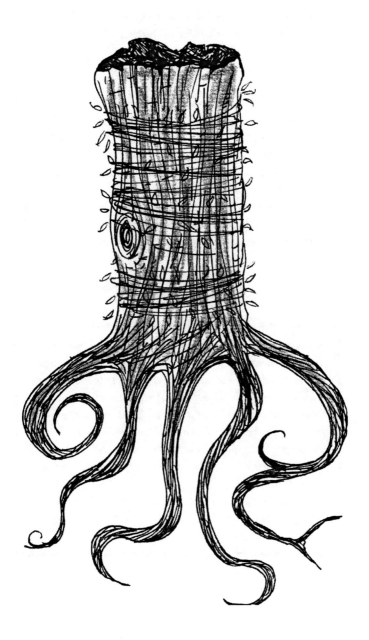

was the coward's victory. His conscience did not feel clean until he was washed in Christ's water at Dorchester – in AD 636 – the same year he died.

To this hill of victory he was brought and to his kin and men a barrow raised.

Here, beneath this very mound, the Barrow King remains until his might is needed again. While he sleeps the grass grows on his back; trees guard his bed – Cwichelmslaewe it was called, in the old tongue. Time wears down words as they are rolled about in the mouths of men, like well-thumbed coins, and over the years it became known as Scutchamer Knob.

The tellers would fall silent then, ending with a toast to the King under the Hill for luck. It's wise to keep the dead happy. They like to hear tales of themselves. They are good listeners.

Scutchamer Knob was excavated in 1842 in a rather brutal fashion, hence its current crescent moon shape. The dig discovered the moot-stake – an oaken stump bound with willow twigs. Cwichelm existed and gets several mentions in The Anglo-Saxon Chronicles. *He was a king of the Gewisse – a people in the upper Thames area who later created the kingdom of Wessex. The market at the barrow did used to take place, and the local belief was Cwichelm was buried there. He joins an exalted company of chthonic kings, including, of course, King Arthur. It was a meeting place and a place of magic and still has a strange atmosphere to this day. From these scraps I have stitched together this tale.*

Thirty-five

OLD SCRAT IN OXFORDSHIRE

The Devil, or Old Scrat as he's known around these parts, liked to visit Oxfordshire as much as any county in the land. For some reason, he took a special shine to North Leigh. It was a well-known fact in the area that Hill Farm was haunted by the Lord of the Flies himself – as well as having more than its fair share of ghosts – despite having a priest's hole in it (although perhaps the priests themselves perpetuated the legend to keep unwanted visitors away). One man who lived there became suddenly rich and it was commonly believed he had found the 'ghosts' treasure'. Another local, Jack Adams, claimed to have seen Old Scrat himself by Hill Farm, describing him as 'all spotted and speckled', so the saying arose locally: 'all spotted and speckled like Jack Adam's Devil'.

Old Scrat was fond of appearing to North Leigh Sabbath-breakers. If anyone went a-nutting on a Sunday, he went with them, helping them by pulling down the branches within easy reach. At the water-pump, the old wives would mutter: 'Nutting is always a chancy past-time and those young girls do indulge in it to the hazard of their maidenhood!'

One day, some men caught a badger and put him in a sack, but on the way home it disappeared, leaving a strong smell of brimstone – so even old Brock was accused of being Old Nick.

Once, some boys were playing Sunday cricket on the common when a stranger appeared and offered to join in – he was an excellent player, but at the end of the game, he vanished in a puff of smoke.

In the churchyard there's a tomb with a hole in it on the north side of the church – the Devil's side (most churches have a Devil's gate on that side, look next time and you'll spot one). Anyone foolish enough to run around it twelve times and look through the hole – well, what do you think they will see? Old Scrat peeping back at them, of course!

Sometimes, he appears to you when you don't want him to. Once, a man was walking from North Leigh to Barnard Gate, when the Devil came to him in the shape of a fiery serpent – wrapping itself around him and trapping him for hours. When he was finally able to escape he ran back to North Leigh to get help. He returned with a group of men to the very spot he had been pinned down: 'Here it was, right here!' but the serpent had long disappeared. He's a slippery customer, Old Scrat!

A similar thing happened to a couple of fellows in Swinbrook. Drinking buddies, they were walking back from The Swan Inn, up along the lonely back lane that crosses Ninety Cut Hill. It was a bright moonlit night, the stars were out and their spirits were high. They were having a good old chat, when for some reason they both fell silent at the same time and came to a dead stop. Before them was something jet black and about the height of a piano. Then it changed into a column about the height and shape of a man, a man made of smoke. Frozen in terror, they watched as it moved in a zigzag motion before them, first this way, then that, like a frightened dog – though the men were the ones whimpering. It seemed to want to get by. One of the men pulled out a torch and flashed it at the thing, but there was nothing there, only withered undergrowth by the roadside. Laughing nervously, the men carried on. Later, they discussed it, safe and snug inside, and agreed they had seen the same thing. One reckoned it was a ghost but the wiser of the two knew who it was alright: Old Scrat, that's who!

But Old Scrat gets some bad press – sometimes he wants to help. Take for example the three churches of Adderbury, Bloxham and King's Sutton, famed for their elegant spires – the tallest parish churches in the county. They were built by three masons who were brothers; Old Scrat turned up to give them a hand as a labourer. The brothers kept him busy, running back and forth. He got tired, and one day he fell down with a load of mortar and so made Crouch Hill. An old saying goes:

Bloxham for length,
Adderbury for strength,
and King's Sutton for beauty.

Nobody thanks Old Scrat for them. There's no sympathy for the Devil in Oxfordshire.

Bloxham Spire

These three spires are not unique in encountering devilish building problems. St Mary's Church in Ambrosden, south-east of Bicester, has a siting legend attached to it. Every morning when the stonemasons returned to the field, in which the church was being built, they would find the stones to have mysteriously moved to another site. Eventually, after happening on a number of occasions, the workmen gave up and built the church where the stones reappeared. The Devil was thought to be the prime suspect. Old Scrat is a frequent visitor to other counties, notably Wiltshire and Gloucestershire, where a kind of satanic song-line has been surveyed through the folk tales. He is often 'blamed' for ancient sites (interpreted in acknowledgement of their pagan origins). Unusually, here it is for God's own house.

Thirty-six

FRIAR BACON AND THE BRAZEN HEAD

Friar Bacon was renowned for his learning; there was nobody in thirteenth-century Britain who knew more than him (or so he liked to think). He claimed to know the secrets of Heaven and Earth and perhaps even Hell, so was rumoured to be a magician. This was not without foundation, but perhaps what is magic for one age is merely the science of a future one. Maybe Friar Bacon was just ahead of his time and simply knew more than his contemporaries?

Yet, even the mightiest magician has to start somewhere.

As a boy, Bacon was something of a prodigy. He came from a West Country farming family. His father could see his son was bright, a genius even, but didn't want him to go to Oxford. As long as he had learning enough to use his father's hard-earned wealth wisely, he'd be happy. But Bacon gave his father the slip and ran away to a cloister to study further. Showing great promise, he was invited to hone his scholarly pursuits at the university in Oxford. Thrilled, he set off for the City of Dreaming Spires, where he 'perfected himself in all the sciences', becoming a master of the secrets of art and nature. He set up residence in Oxford and so began his extraordinary career.

Friar Bacon's cunning art was in great demand. He had some powerful patrons, including Prince Edward, son and heir of King Henry III. With Friar Bacon's help, Edward seduced the Fair Maid of Fressingfield. The Friar sent an emissary on the Prince Regent's behalf – Lacy – who ended up falling in love with Margaret. Bacon showed his patron that they planned to wed in secret, through a 'magic viewing glass', which Bacon interrupted with his sorcery.

Another time, the King and Queen were sojourning in Oxfordshire, when they sent for this increasingly famous scholar, via a messenger. Friar Bacon agreed to come and said he would be there two hours before the messenger; and further, he would also reveal the name of the wench the page had just been with! Flushing red, the page left and Friar Bacon slowly packed a case and set off, whistling, at a casual pace. When he arrived at the Royal residence, he was commanded by the King and Queen to show them his art. Reluctant at first, he conjured dancers and musicians, clowns and acrobats, a great feast, and finally exotic perfumes – dazzling all fives senses. The King and Queen were impressed and rewarded him richly. As he left, showered in gold, the page arrived all muddy and breathless. Friar Bacon conjured before him his sweetheart – a greasy kitchen-maid – much to the amusement of the court.

This was only one of Bacon's many accomplishments. He famously defeated a German magician called Vandemast before the rulers of Europe, after which they all sought his services.

And so Friar Bacon grew in wealth and influence. But he was not without his own Achilles' Heel.

Friar Bacon had a servant, Miles, who seemed as witless as his master was wise, and often hindered when he should assist – getting in the way of his many experiments. Clumsy and incompetent Miles – why did he keep him on? He wondered himself sometimes!

Friar Bacon had a professional rival – Friar Bungay, a scholar educated at Oxford and Cambridge and a member of the Order of Friars Minor. Bungay matched Bacon in learning and they were notorious for arguing over philosophical points. And yet, there was an underlying fondness between them – there was no one else who Bacon could feel was his equal.

Together, they planned Bacon's most daring experiment yet – a mechanical head of brass, which would protect the shores of Britain with a wall of brass. It would be able to speak and warn of danger; the ultimate in state-of-the-art medieval security. They laboured long and hard at this and the task was made twice as hard by Bacon and Bungay bickering over each and every technical point. They tinkered and bickered until Bacon could not take it anymore and he sent Bungay away – too many chefs spoil the broth! He was fed up of Bungay flagging up yet another design flaw. It was nearly complete; each piece of the mechanical head had been exquisitely crafted to the smallest of measurements. He wasn't going to rebuild it. It had taken over a year to build already. Time was slipping away. Every day, Friar Bacon felt wearier and wearier, his naps getting longer and longer.

Friar Bacon, exhausted, slept in his lab. He had not properly rested for days, but his masterpiece was complete: the Brazen Head would guard the coast of the kingdom with an ever-waking mechanical gaze – the ultimate fire-wall.

Yet the Brazen Head watched with amber eyes – eyes that glowed with a strange intelligence. It seemed to see beyond the coast of Britain; beyond the cold seas that encircled it; beyond the shores of the Earth itself – into the past and into the future. It heated up and steam poured from its vents. It shook and the whole lab trembled, yet still Friar Bacon did not wake from his deep slumber. Miles the servant watched on in horror – hapless and helpless, he did not think to stir his master as the Brazen Head spoke: 'Time is…' its metallic voice rang out. More steam poured from it, the eyes glowed brighter and it spoke a second time, brass words bouncing off the stone walls: 'Time was…' Silence settled, the head stopped shaking, then it erupted into motion, whirring and clattering, and spoke one last time: 'Time is Past…' it boomed, with a hollow, metallic voice, before finally smashing to smithereens on the floor – coils and cogs everywhere.

Miles turned pale, looking at the broken head.

Friar Bacon awoke to a scene of chaos and devastation. He blazed at his useless servant – why didn't he wake him! May he be damned to Hell! 'Get out of my sight,' he roared. 'And do not come back!'

Friar Bacon kicked the useless brass skull across the floor, stubbing his toe. Cursing in pain, he slumped into a chair, head in his hands. All his efforts were in vain. Perhaps he had over-reached himself. His heart had lost its fire.

The lab was eventually cleared up. Friar Bacon was bankrupt, having poured all of his resources into the project, and so he took on a final job – two Oxonian students came to him, concerned about their fathers, who had vowed to duel each other to the death the next day over some foolish matter of honour. Friar Bacon could not stop this and duelling etiquette meant that they could not attend, but he could show them the duel through his magic glass. A morbid curiosity compelled the students to look into the crystal ball. The Oxonians watched in horror as their fathers' slew each other before their very eyes. Fuelled by grief and rage, the students turned on each other and did the same before the magician could stop them. Stunned, he looked down at the two slowly cooling corpses, mirroring the two in the glass.

He was so horrified by this that Friar Bacon renounced all magic. He burnt all his books – ancient, priceless magical tomes containing all of his learning. And he turned back to God, living out his last few years in devout contemplation.

His servant, Miles, was said to receive his diabolical punishment – riding to Hell on the Devil's back, and becoming a tapster in Hell, serving the endless thirst of demons.

Wherever they ended up, perhaps both souls might now have a better idea what the Brazen Head's prophesy meant: time is; time was; and time is past.

Friar Bacon is Oxfordshire's own Doctor Faustus, and yet he does not seem to be in league with the Devil, as one of the many tales illustrates…

There was a prodigal gentleman of Oxfordshire who brought his estate into ruin. In desperation he borrowed money from an old 'penny-father', who turned out to be the Devil himself. The interest on his loan was his very soul. He turns to Friar Bacon, who agrees to help. They meet the Devil in a wood and Friar Bacon acts as judge. He outwits the Devil and drives him away, freeing the man from his contract. Lacking a Mephistopheles, the Germanic magician Vandermast seems to have been Bacon's arch-enemy and this epic feud warrants a whole story in itself (at its climax, Bacon's professional rival, Bungay, and Vandermast kill each other). These magical morality tales seem to be part of a whole sub-genre. Do they refer to one scholarly magician or several – perhaps reflecting the lay persons fear of 'too much learning'. Are the concerns about state-of-the-art research in Oxford (Dawkins et al) a modern equivalent?

Thirty-seven

THE
CAVALIER ROOM

Ensconced snugly in the verdant flanks of the Cotswolds is the elegant Jacobean mansion of Chastleton. Just off the old Fosseway, down a winding narrow lane to the brow of a hill – there it sits by its own church, where birds sing in the Spring sun and the silent dead push up the snowdrops. Walk amongst these ancient ivy-covered tombs beneath the penumbral yews and you get a sense of the many lives that have lived and died within its influence. It has known famous and infamous sons. Here is the tale of one – and a lady of exceptional character.

Chastleton has always been a Royalist house; built in 1612, by Walter Jones, a wool merchant of Witney, it prospered on the fat of the land. Its lush meadows and grounds provided a safe haven for the cultivation of crops and the rearing of livestock – and the occasional fleeing war refugee!

During the Civil War it gave refuge to an Arthur Jones, grand-son of Walter Jones, who had escaped from the defeat at Worcester on the 3rd of September 1651.

Later that night, after a thirty-mile ride, the exhausted and anxious Arthur appeared, his poor horse in a sorry state. His lath-ered steed was rubbed down and stabled and its rider given food,

refreshing draughts and refuge. In one of the bedrooms, called
the Cavalier Room, is a secret chamber hidden behind the arras
that lined the room. Arthur was hidden here, and just in time!
Suddenly, there was the sound of horses' hooves echoing down the
lane – his Roundhead pursuers had arrived.

Hidden in his bolt-hole, Arthur's heart began to beat faster as he
heard down below the firm banging of gauntlet on wood. 'Open in
the name of Parliament!' a stern voice bellowed.

Mrs Jones let them in as her servants stabled their horses.
Without a 'by-your-leave' from the Lady of the Manor, the grim
Roundheads searched the house. Fearing they would do more harm
left to themselves, Mrs Jones took matters in hand and led the party
of soldiers from room to room. In their Northampton-made boots
they tramped through the house, pulling back arras and turning
over mattresses. No cupboard or wardrobe was left undisturbed.

With an expressionless face she showed them every room. The Captain carefully watched for a reaction, a clue – but her mask gave nothing away.

They hunted for the rarest of game, a 'Royal stag' – the fleeing King himself – or so they thought.

Finally, they came to the Cavalier Room and searched it thoroughly. Mrs Jones feigned nonchalance as the Captain scrutinised her.

Arthur kept silent behind the screen, terrified of making a noise and being discovered.

Finally, they finished. 'Nothing, sir.'

The Captain gritted his teeth.

'Would your men be wanting a bed for the night?' the Lady of the Manor asked, the ghost of a smile on her lips.

'Yes,' barked the Captain. 'We'll take this room. Send up some supper.'

'As you wish, Captain. I hope you'll find the accommodation to your liking.'

Mrs Jones fixed their refreshment herself, mixing laudanum with their wine. She had a servant bring it up on a tray.

The soldiers were thirsty after their day of battle and hard-ride. They knocked the wine back, their boorish laughter echoing through the house. For a while, it was unbearably noisy. Then it fell strangely quiet.

Mrs Jones ventured upstairs to the Cavalier Room. The door was ajar and from within she could hear loud snoring. Sprawled across the room were the whole company – fast asleep.

'Sweet dreams, Captain,' smiled Mrs Jones.

She gave the all clear and one of the tapestries twitched. Timidly, her son appeared. She placed a finger to her lips, and then signalled for him to follow. Tiptoeing between the sleeping soldiers, Arthur Jones slipped away before his mother led him, business-like, to the stables.

'Take one of the horses and ride as far away as it will carry you.'

'But, what about you...?'

'Don't worry about me. I can handle them. Go!'

Arthur reluctantly mounted the fastest looking horse and blew his mother a kiss, before digging in his heels. With a whinny, the horse burst from the stable and galloped into the night.

In the morning, the soldiers awoke, groggily, to discover one of their horses mysteriously absent, and their 'Royal' prey vanished like the dew.

The Captain roared at her.

'The horse, where is it?'

Mrs Jones feigned innocence. 'Perhaps you misplaced it, like your wits.'

'Lady, you overstep your mark!'

'Why sir, if you cannot handle yor wine, whose fault is that but your own?'

The Captain clenched his fist. 'You will pay for harbouring a wanted criminal!'

'Lower yourself to threaten a woman if you must – such is the greatness of your cause – but may I remind you that all the while your Royal stag is getting away…'

The Captain glared at her. 'Men, saddle up. We ride.'

'Farewell, Captain. I would like to say what a pleasure it's been having you as my guest…'

Furious, they galloped off.

They never caught Arthur, and the Lady of the Manor survived the Civil War with her splendid demesne intact. And so, Chastleton House still stands to this day, in all its glory – a deceptively peaceful corner of England.

Chastleton House was sold to the Jones' by a certain Robert Catesby. It would appear he used the sale of the property to help fund the notorious Gunpowder Plot. So, its fortunes have been balanced between Parliament and Crown. Somehow it has survived the vicissitudes of history, and these days' looks like the very bastion of English respectability and peaceful, well-heeled status quo, sitting comfortably in its leafy vale. Yet the walls remember the time the Lady of the Manor hid a 'Royal stag' and defied the Puritan Lord Protector, Cromwell.

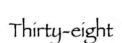

Thirty-eight

THE ANGEL OF THE THAMES

Old Father Thames they call me; a strong brown god – how wrong the poets were; how right. Look at me snaking sluggishly through London, like a bloated anaconda – one that had swallowed a city, and it would be easy to agree. Silently, I carry the sins of the citizens; receive them all like a brown-robed priest taking confession, offering forgiveness and sometimes sprinkling them with blessings – showing them a glimpse of grace.

In recent years, there have been several sightings of me: a TV presenter, on camera, caught a glimpse; a group of Korean students posing for a photograph; day-trippers; dog-walkers; down-and-outs; and the high and mighty. All are ignored or mocked with laughter. They say they are seeing what they want to see. They have seen the dodgy footage on You-Tube, on questionable websites, and convinced themselves that that flash of light caught in the corner of the eye, that faint smudge in the background of a holiday snap, that blink-and-you-miss-it blur on the shaky camcorder shot, is an angel. It is easy to see why sceptical folk scorn such digital delusions. An urban myth, the folklorist might call me: a psychologist's field day.

They do not hear my screams. They do not hear a river crying. My beautiful smooth body filled with your toxic waste, your sewage, your oil. What once flowed clear – innocent as Spring – from its source, turned dark with the silt of humanity, so that I fulfil my name, 'dark flow'. Once, in Victorian times, I became so polluted that the Houses of Parliament were closed down: the Great Stink, it was named. Ironic, since it is usually from Westminster – the fording place – that such noisome odours emerged.

I was dying.

But nature can be kind, and several severe winters killed off the diseases that ravaged me. I froze and they held Frost Fairs on me – stalls and side-shows offering every kind of gewgaw and mountebank, great marquees filled with Nine-day Wonders, sled-rides and spit-roasts, imagine! Children, playing in my garden. My heart melted and I forgave them.

I am old; I have seen too much to hold on to anything for long. It is all water under the bridge.

Forgive me. I am prone to meander. Occasionally, in my superannuated twilight, the estuary of my existence, I have been known to bitter outbursts.

But once I was young and sprightly.

Let me take you back to my beginning, to my source.

In a peaceful meadow in Gloucestershire I begin, quietly and modestly. Like a shy maiden I can only be glimpsed fleetingly. My waters rise at certain times of the year. Thames Head they call it. There's a stone there – like a gravestone in reverse, marking my birth. Once there was a grand statue there of Old Father Thames but this has been moved downriver, which feels more fitting, to St John's Lock, near Lechlade, the highest point to which I am navigable. Beyond that, I remain a chaste maiden. No barges penetrate my leafy secrets. I am deflowered by commerce soon enough, but for a while I remain a virgin river – nay, a mere stream, like a strip of a girl, all knees and pigtails, awkward in her own body – before I become a womanly river. Appropriate, despite what I later become known as, for above where my cousin the River Thame joins me, a mere forty miles old (in Dorchester, Oxfordshire) I was known for centuries by gazetteers and cartographers as the Isis – a suitable name for an English Nile perhaps – an ancient name for the oldest stretch of me. Until half a million years ago this was my original course; then I flowed north-east to flow out into the sea at Ipswich. Well, when I say sea I mean the North Sea Basin. Then, I joined others to form the Channel River, among them the Rhine. But ice and flood made me change my ways. The great flood came, and the North Sea cut me off from my continental family tree.

And never the twain shall meet again.

Although dwarfed by my Egyptian sister and other siblings around the world, I am still the longest river in England (not quite Britain – that honour goes to big sis, Sabrina) and similarly prone to flooding. Indeed, some speculate the name the Celts gave me, Tamesas, means just this; the Darkly Flowing One. Was I once a Celtic goddess? They venerated water and believed rivers and springs were inhabited by spirits. Well, put Thame and Isis together and you have Thamesis, or eventually, Thames. And yet 'Tamesis' is a Greek girl's name – for a goddess of the river.

I was rather fond of the Celts; they loved to offer me gifts: swords, knives, shields, coins, as well as their shining words. They gave me their prayers and blessings, wishes and curses. They fought to defend me – tattooed warriors; the thought of them gives me a thrill! Just saying their names brings a shiver to my spine: the Catuvellauni, the Atrebates, the Dobunni…

Then those tin men came, wanting to conquer it all. And many others followed: Vikings; Saxons; Normans. Fighting bloody battles by my banks; building castles to control me. All were conquered in the end by the land – settling down, raising crops and families. In the soft rain and mists of this island, their fierce blood cooled and they learned to love more than hate; to value life more than death.

Then came the trade – eel-trapping; willow-cutting; milling; fishing – and with it the traffic. Timber and wool, foodstuffs and livestock were carried on barges down from Oxford, as well as stone from the Cotswolds to rebuild St Paul's after the Great Fire. Life got busy on the river – I became one of the busiest water-ways in the world, one of the busiest ports, the hub of an Empire. I was the main artery of English life – 'liquid history' I have been called: history happened in, on and around me. English law was forged on one of my islands – Runnymede, where King John and the barons signed the Magna Carta in 1215. At Oxford the dreaming spires were raised and great minds were nurtured. Along my banks palaces fit for royalty were fashioned at Hampton Court, Kew, Richmond-on-Thames, Whitehall and Greenwich. The elite were weaned at Windsor and Eton. I carried kings and queens to their coronations at Westminster and executions at the Tower. Swans glided up and down me. Poets rhapsodised. Novelists took my dark water and turned it into ink; composers, into symphonies; artists, into light. All communed with my spirit, just as those Celts had done.

As, occasionally, the unsuspecting sightseer does.

The dancing patterns on the water are mesmerising, but beware! My beauty can be deadly, it can madden, and it can lead men to do insane things. It can lure them to their doom. And if I am not placated, if I am exploited, I can take a deadly toll. Many have been taken in my chill embrace. 'Thames runs chill twixt mead and hill,' it is said. How true.

On September 3rd 1878, I claimed my deadliest price, when the crowded pleasure boat *Princess Alice* collided with Bywell Castle, killing over 640 souls. In 1989, fifty-one party-goers drowned when the *Marchioness* was struck by a dredger. They were celebrating the birthday of a merchant banker; city-types; Thatcher's children. Boom and bust, and down their ship of fools went.

Some say I have a cold heart. But by the time I have reached the capital I have been polluted, controlled, exploited and chartered. So, corrupted by the evil kings of this world, they hold me up as their own dark mirror and see an ancient patriarch. So perhaps you can forgive me if I turn bitter. Yet I have a bottomless heart. I embrace all who come to me – in the womb of death. Mother Thames. Your angel of mercy.

Come to me.

I based this story upon the recent sightings of the 'Angel of the Thames', an article by Robert Goodman, and my own research into the lore of the river. However sceptical one might be about such sightings, it is too tantalising for a storyteller to pass up. Although its source is in Gloucestershire and its estuary in Outer London, it is a prominent feature of Oxfordshire and I found it intriguing that it was often referred to as the Isis above Winchester-upon-Thames. It might seem far-fetched to conceive of a river 'changing sex', but since the British Celts saw the guardian spirits of the water as female (as in Sabrina of the Severn; and Sul of Aquae Sulis), it seems likely that 'Tamesis' was as well. Also, it has been noted that pollution in rivers can cause fish to change sex – it is perhaps using poetic license to extend this to the actual rivers themselves, but why not? Stranger things happen at sea.

Thirty-nine

TAPROOM TALES

The Farmer and the Firkin

There was a lazy, hard-drinking man who never lifted a finger to pitch in, unless it was harvesting time – when the farmer sent out a firkin of cider for the labourers, then he was the first to slake his thirst, hanging around out of turn.

They used to send him out to the middle-o'-field under everyone's eye, however, when he thought no one was looking, stooping by the stooks, he would sneak back to the hedge for a sly swig. The other workers got pretty tired of this and hid the firkin, but he sneaked round and found it, and when they were all busy he ran off with it.

He'd had a good skinful already, so he made for the woods and lay down on the turf-side of a mound that had a hawthorn on it; a fairy thorn. He yawned – whether it was the sun, the cider, or the spell of the place, he soon found himself very drowsy.

Well, it was a nice enough spot to have a quick nap. Twenty winks, then, and he'd be back to work. All of a sudden he saw something small and green by the bank, then another, and then another, and then a whole crowd – pretty little folk, dancing

around him, until they made him dizzy. He wanted to reach out
and shoo them away, but somehow he couldn't move; then, in a
flash, he was alone and could move, so he did.

He picked up the firkin for a long swig. 'Funny dream I had,' he
said, 'all about … nothing.'

And the little voices all round twittered back at him, 'And that's
what you'll find in the firkin!'

This story was collected by Ruth Tongue, who heard it from a
nurse in Middlesex hospital, who had been told it in her student
days by a fellow student from Oxfordshire – who in her turn had
heard it from her grandfather, an Oxfordshire farmer, about his
own farm, in about 1900.

THE DON AND THE LANDLORD

Once in Bibury, in the Colne Valley, an Oxford student offered to teach the landlord of The Swan Inn how to draw strong and mild ale out of the same cask.

'Mild and strong? Out of the same cask? It cannot be done!'

'I shall show you. First I need an auger.'

One was fetched and the student drilled a hole near the bottom of the cask and told the landlord to stop it with his finger. Then he drilled another at the top of the cask and asked him to do the same with his other hand. 'Oh, I've forgotten the spiggots!' said the student. 'Hold on a minute and I'll just go and fetch them.' He went out of the inn, got on his horse and rode away.

The landlord waited patiently at first. 'What is taking that lad?' He called out. No reply. He called again, and once again was met with silence. Growing a bit concerned – what if he had fallen or worse? – the landlord tried to wriggle free but was stuck firm. He called out, growing redder in the face. That student has pulled a prank on him! Luckily, another customer overheard and, much to the landlord's embarrassment, relieved him of his prison. The landlord rose in fury, his face purple, and cursed after the student – who was long gone.

But the landlord had the best of it in the end. So many people came to laugh at him and his gullibility that his trade doubled – more than compensating for the ribbings he took. Since then, the landlord thought twice before listening to the 'wisdom of students'.

There must be many such tales showing the long-term feud between town and gown. In some it is a canny local who gets one over on the gullible student. 'The Oxfordshire Scholar' ballad shows how many students were thought of as irresponsible and overly fond of alcohol. Not much has changed!

Forty

THE
RABBIT ROOM

Memorabilia adorns me now – quiet photographs of the legends I once accommodated; a plaque commemorating their presence. Hordes of tourists come to visit; take snaps; film it with their phones; gasping in delight at how tiny the snug is, how quaint. They pretend to enjoy a pint of tepid English beer, the stodgy food. Enthusiasts linger. Writers stay even longer, sitting in the corner – the hallowed corner – trying to imbibe the atmosphere, to capture the ambience. They ponder on literary immortality while trying to ensure a place for their own ink-stained soul in the bardic firmament. Here is as good a spot as any cathedral or mosque. This last homely house, this Prancing Pony, is a wardrobe, a wood between the worlds, a portal to magical lands – to Middle Earth, Perelandra, Narnia, Logres. Once it was the rabbit hole to Wonderland and now it's a knife-cut gateway to Jordan College, to quantum worlds beyond reckoning. The new chap has been in, of course, raised a glass to his antecedents, two fingers to Jack. Perhaps one day they'll be visiting his old haunts? The God-botherers and the pagans; the atheist scholars and the fanatic movie devotees in costume; those who come to pay homage here. To breathe in the same air, well, almost – it no longer swirls with pipe smoke and cigarettes, but the

fire still crackles in the grate; the pumps provide the same local ales; the kitchen still offers its homity pie; the barflies their homilies; and when it's quiet – when the customers don't drown out the silence with their chatter – the voices come back. The ghosts in the wall stir, those lost lunchtimes are replayed – a decade of Tuesdays – recorded like voices from long ago on wax cylinder and reel-to-reel, by the wooden Akashic record of my walls; listen, hear their voices …

J.R.R. Tolkien, pipe-smoker, Received Pronunciation, but at times fast and low; C.S. 'Jack' Lewis, donnish, slight trace of Ulster, at times stentorian; Owen Barfield, solicitor, a softer educated voice; Charles Williams, poet, novelist, occultist, North London accent; and now and then Charles Blagrove, landlord of the Eagle and Child, an Oxfordshire man.

One by one they would share their work and offer gruff, honest feedback. They would share tales from lands far away and, sometimes, closer to home...

Once there was a beautiful Queen who lived in a beautiful house. It had many elegant rooms in which to entertain elegant guests. And even lovelier were the gardens. The parterre had four-and-twenty square beds with Irish yews at the corners; the Italian garden had a large ornamental pool enclosed by yew hedges and set about with statues; beyond was a wild garden, with limetree avenues, shrubs, a stream and pond.

It had not always been so lovely.

When they had inherited this kingdom, her husband, the King, set his servants to work restoring it. It was a difficult time; the country had just gone to War – a land that is always there, waiting for the foolhardy to visit.

Many brave men went to the Land of War and never returned.

The Queen invited her beautiful friends, the Bloomsberries – many of whom did not believe in living by the sword. Some called them Conchies and accused them of cowardice. From the cruel tongues and the consensus madness they came seeking refuge. The bright, the brilliant and the beautiful: philosophers; poets; novelists; peace campaigners; aristocrats and socialists. They had many lovely parties where conversation flowed like champagne. To escape the war they worked on the land. The gardens prospered as the Queen's house became a sanctuary of sanity in an insane world. The Queen took a lover and found happiness.

For a while, all was bliss.

Yet, amongst them was a traitor, a turncoat, who weaselled his way into their hearts until he won their trust and learnt their secrets and then, when he left with their love and praise ringing in his ears, he wrote poisonous things about them. Some say he was blinded; others that he had true sight and saw things as they truly were. A scandalous book was published, mocking them, and the spell of the palace was broken. The parties stopped, the gardens became neglected and overgrown, and the Queen and her husband, the King, moved out.

For a while they had pursued and found happiness. They had held off the barbaric tides with their cultured ways, but they could not fend off the enemy within – the worm in their hearts and the fool who saw.

* * *

The room settled back into its silence. There was a cough.

'I detest allegory,' Tolkien responded with a jab of his pipe.

'At least it didn't have another effing elf in it,' quipped Jack, raising a glass to his old friend. The others pitched in, pulled the tale apart, always with good humour and a deep fondness for one another. Yet somehow, the enchantment remained – lingering in the air like pipe smoke as the conversation flowed.

Mingling with the voices are other sounds: the clink of coin and chink of glasses; laughter; the strike of a match; the puff of a pipe; and the crackle in the grate; the rustle of papers; murmurs of appreciation or snorts of good natured mockery; ripples of warm applause; coughs and scraping of chairs and farewells.

They kept meeting throughout the war – here and at other pubs in the city, unless prevented by 'no beer'. Later in the war, before the D-Day landings, the American soldiers would come and drink the city dry. Yet the Inklings sustained each other from deeper wells, sharing work in progress, making conversation, supporting one another, living by their myths.

Yet man that is born of a woman hath but a short time to live. One of them would die a week after the war ended – yet his brief time with the Inklings left its mark – one of them would find his muse again; another find joy in an unexpected guise; two would rise to fame, but this you know. My story now has ended. But if you chance to visit the city of dreaming spires, pay the Bird and Baby a visit, sit in the Rabbit Room and raise a glass to the Inklings, whose doorways lie open still, waiting for you to enter.

During the thirties and forties, in The Eagle and Child, a pub in Oxford, every Tuesday lunchtime a group of writers who called themselves the Inklings would meet. Amongst them were a couple of Oxford dons who would become two of the most famous writers of the twentieth century, J.R.R. Tolkien and C.S. Lewis, and some less well known authors but equally influential to the group, including Charles Williams. Here, working drafts of The Lord of the Rings, *the Narnia novels and other works of literary importance were read out for the first time.*

Sitting in the Snug Bar, called the Rabbit Room, sipping local ale, one imbibes something of the atmosphere that made the sharing of tales by this group of friends so conducive. It is a numinous place where storytelling, literature and listeners converge – a Mecca for all pilgrims of the imagination.

The embedded tale, which I call The Queen of the Bloomsberries, *was an invented one about the beautiful society hostess Lady Ottoline Morrel, who held famous literary soirees at the lovely Garsington Manor, on the outskirts of Oxford. She was fêted by the Bloomsbury Set – among her elite clique were Bertrand Russell (her lover), Aldous Huxley, Rupert Brooke, and others. The Manor, no doubt, has its fair share of tales to tell too. These days it hosts an annual opera gala – so I'll end this narrative perambulation of the county with a fat lady singing.*

BIBLIOGRAPHY

Books

Briggs, Katherine M., *A Sample of British Folk-Tales*, (Routledge & Kegan, 1977)

Briggs, Katherine M., *The Folklore of the Cotswolds*, (Batsford, 1974)

Carpenter, Humphrey, *The Inklings*, (Ballantine, 1981)

Crossley-Holland, Kevin, *Folk-Tales of the British Isles*, (Faber & Faber, 1991)

Evans, Herbert A., *Highways & Byways in Oxford & the Cotswolds*, (Macmillan, 1924)

Falkner, John Mead, *A Pocket Guide to Oxforshire*, (1894)

Foss, Michael, ed., *Folk Tales of the Britsh Isles*, (Book Club Associates, 1987)

Gantz, Jeffrey, *The Mabinogion*, (Penguin Classics, 1976)

Grimm, Jacob and Wilhelm, *Grimms' Fairy Tales*

Lewis-Jones, June, *Folklore of the Cotswolds*, (Tempus, 2003)

Marshall, R.M., *Oxfordshire Byways*, (Alden Press, Oxford, 1935)

Millson, Cecilia, *Tales of Old Oxfordshire*, (Countryside Books, 1983)

Westwood, Jennifer, *Albion: A Guide to Legendary Britain*, (Book Club Associates, 1986)

Williams, Alfred, *Folk Songs of the Upper Thames*, (Duckworth, 1922/1971)

Journals & Other Publications

Eastwood, David, 'Communities, Protest and Police in Early Nineteenth-Century Oxfordshire: The Enclosure of Otmoor Reconsidered', *The Agricultural History Review*, Vol. 44, No. 1, British Agricultural History Society (1996) pp. 35-46

Goodman, Robert, 'Legend of the Thames', *Paranormal*, No.49 (July 2010)

Inman, Peggy, 'Amy Robsart and Cumnor Place', Cumnor History Society

Readers Digest, *Folklore: Myths and Legends of Britain* (1973)

'Singing Histories: Oxfordshire', taken from Sing London (www.singlondon.org)

Spears, James E., *The 'Boar's Head Carol' and Folk Tradition Folklore*, Vol. 85, No. 3. (1974) pp. 194-198

INDEX

If you enjoyed this book, you may also be interested in ...

Gloucestershire Folk Tales
Anthony Nanson
This collection of tales includes sky-ships over Bristol, the silk-caped wraith of Dover's Hill, and the snow foresters on the Cotswolds, as well as stories of the days of Sabrina, spirit of the Severn, and the Nine Hags of Gloucester.
978 0 7524 6017 8

Nottinghamshire Folk Tales
Pete Castle
Ranging from the silly to the gory and unsettling, this collection features tales of love, murder, and all kinds of roguery, from historical to fabled – including an array of heroes and villains.
978 0 7524 6377 3

Wiltshire Folk Tales
Kirsty Hartsiotis
Discover Merlin's trickery, King Alfred's bravery, dab-chicks and the devil, the flying monk of Malmesbury and the ravenous maggot of Little Langford – no stone is left unturned to discover the roots of the county.
978 0 7524 5736 9

Visit our website and discover thousands of other History Press books.

www.thehistorypress.co.uk

Lightning Source UK Ltd.
Milton Keynes UK
UKOW02f0656111214

242934UK00001B/2/P